Becoming a Chief Home Officer

HEARTS AT HOME® WORKSHOP SERIES

FOREWORD BY CHARLENE ANN BAUMBICH

Becoming a Chief Home Officer

THRIVING IN YOUR "CAREER SHIFT" TO STAY-AT-HOME MOM

WITH LEADER'S GUIDE AND PERSONAL REFLECTIONS

Allie Pleiter

ZONDERVAN™

GRAND RAPIDS, MICHIGAN 49530 USA

ZONDERVAN™

Becoming a Chief Home Officer
Copyright © 2002 by Alyse Stanko Pleiter

Requests for information should be addressed to:

Zondervan, *Grand Rapids, Michigan 49530*

Library of Congress Cataloging-in-Publication Data

Pleiter, Allie, 1962-
  Becoming a chief home officer : thriving in your career shift to stay–at–home mom / Allie Pleiter.
    p. cm. – (Hearts at home workshop series)
  Includes bibliographical references and index.
  ISBN 0-310-23742-4 (softcover)
  1. Mothers–United States. 2. Housewives–United States. 3. Motherhood–United States. 4. Parenting–United States. I. Title. II. Series.
HQ759.P565 2002
306.874'3 – dc21

                          2002004258

Published in association with Yates & Yates, LLP, Attorneys and Counselors, Suite 1000, Literary Agent, Orange, CA.

Interior design by Susan Ambs

Printed in the United States of America

02 03 04 05 06 /❖ DC/ 10 9 8 7 6 5 4 3 2 1

In memory of my mother,
Etta Stanko,
the original Lady in Charge

contents

Foreword by
Charlene Baumbich

PARENTING: GLORIOUS CUDDLES and sleeping babes. Brilliant grades and "Always plays nice with friends. Great job, Mom!" on report cards. After bouts of prayer and discussion, you toss your pantyhose, rolodex, and business suits aside to don your Stay-At-Home Mom of the Century banner with pride ... in your dreams.

Parenting reality: Eyes snapping open at 2 A.M. Groan. Weary-boned from wiping the endless runny noses of never-sleeping kids and yourself. Tapped out funds and distressing teacher conferences. "Messy and missing papers. Doesn't listen well." (Oh, like that's a news bulletin!) And if someone evaluated you, what would they say? "Messy house, doesn't play nice with her own children, waffles between glazed over and ear-piercing banshee."

Welcome to Parenting Flunky 101. How did such an intelligent, competent business woman end up so pitifully ... lost? And to think, you—like Allie—made the difficult but deliberate (doink!) decision to quit your successful career and stay home with your child!

Then again, maybe parenting is all you ever wanted and everything that proceeded it was just a warm-up and preparation—or so you thought. Or maybe you've been a stay-at-home mom for years, but just this moment decided Runaway Mom sounds like a better title. Now what?!

Like my dad used to say, you're just in a little period of transition. My friend Allie Pleiter is masterful at letting you know you are not alone. No, you are, as she says, partnered with God in "shaping destiny one child at a time." (Yowza!) And at the same time you are, as is she, a sister traveler—colleague, if you will—on this oft-times lost road of parenting. But Allie has grace-filledly found her way—again and again—and here she is posting light rays to help you find yours.

I am deliriously proud to be the one who gets to ready you for her quick-read, fun (laugh out loud), revelation (THANK YOU, Jesus), honest (I can't believe she admitted that), energizing (I know I can, I know I can...), affirming (what you do has value), spiritually deepening (probing questions), and most importantly, take-it-to-the-mat usable stories, ideas, and inspiration.

You can not only transition and survive, but you can become the Chief Home Officer (CHO) of your home using the business principles she delivers. Allie frees you to prioritize self care, introduces you to the wisdom of granting a Slug Day, inspires you to wear sassy under-wear, and motivates you to become an adaptable, coping, spontaneous, creative, roll-with-the-punches, inspired, humble, and joy-filled model for your kids to emulate.

"CHO! CHO! CHO!" Just see if you aren't chanting this by the time you're done reading!

Acknowledgments

MY FIRST AND highest thanks go to my Lord for working with this all-too-stubborn clay to mold it to his amazing purpose. I am daily thankful for God's wisdom, guidance, and counsel, and for the privilege of sharing my thoughts with each of you.

My husband, Jeff, deserves heaps upon heaps of gratitude for enduring things far outside the bounds of standard matrimony. For smiling and nodding at my non-stop gush of . . . well, my non-stop gush. Not every man can calmly support a wife who reinvents herself thrice in one marriage (and I imagine I'm hardly done yet). If I am capable of flashes of brilliance, it is because of the quiet, solid foundation he provides. I am also grateful to my children for all they have taught me, and for their unparalleled ability to give me "material."

To the women of Yorkfield Presbyterian Church, especially the women of Mothership and W.I.N.G.S., for their fellowship, wisdom, humor . . . and food. To Becky, who taught me much of what I know about good mothering and great friendship. To Christina, Charlene, and Martha for coming alongside, coming before, and coming after me in motherhood. To the women of Hearts at Home for their vision, their faith, and their tireless commitment to ministry. To the dozens of women everywhere over my lifetime who gave me bits and pieces of their lives, their experience, and their advice. It may take a village to raise a child, but it takes a legion of good women to raise a mother.

It has been my highest privilege to pen these words. God's richest blessings to each and every one of you.

chapter 7

Consider Yourself Promoted

THE WORLD'S MOST unlikely at-home mother?
That's me.

I never planned—and hardly expected—to make the journey from working mother to stay-at-home mother.

You know how there are some women who are just seeping home and hearth from their very pores? You just look at them and you smell freshly baked cookies. Those are the good moms at home, I thought.

I was not one of those. Not even close.

Oh, if my preconceptions could see me now! Don't get me wrong, I'm still not a home-and-hearth wizard, but I *am* a thriving, growing, enjoying-not-every-moment-but-awfully-close kind of mom. God seems to specialize in such astounding transformations. Women like me—successful working moms who chose to leave their careers behind for a new job description—abound in parks and nursery schools everywhere these days. Although I felt like it at first, I am far from alone. Just the fact that you are reading these words bears testimony to the growing numbers of women who are undertaking the same journey from the workplace to managing a home.

Some of you may have yearned for this all your life—you've been just itching to be a mother at home. Others of you may feel you are as unlikely candidates as I. Or perhaps you are somewhere in between. The astounding news is that it doesn't matter what your background looks like. The path to becoming a stay-at-home mom is as unique and individual as each one of us. No matter your age, stage in life, geography, or biography, all of us are recreating ourselves. We are all in this messy, scary business of reshaping our values and lives to focus on the home front together.

Someone once said, "The shortest trip between two points is with good company." I heartily agree. Any journey benefits from companions (with the possible exception of several preschoolers in a minivan). Even if you can't see anyone on the road with you, it is still comforting to know that others have gone before you. If you are lucky, they have left signs of their journey and hints to ease your own.

These pages are my hints to you.

The Girl Least Likely To

Me? At home? Are you asking yourself that? I sure was.

I found staying at home a *very scary* concept. Images of chenille bathrobes and dust mops danced in my head. *Housewife.* I didn't think I could do this. The sleek working woman was what I knew. Still, the lure to spend my energy on my family, to make *them* my career, grew to be as irresistible as it seemed irrational. I was sure I was not cut out for this sort of thing.

Truth be told, I had a very positive experience as a working mother. God was kind enough to give me a good-natured baby as our firstborn, and I felt as if I had successfully grafted motherhood into my life, work, and personality without too much struggle. I linked my home computer up to the office and was known to carry on more than one business call with a suckling infant in my arms. I learned to hand express breast milk after enduring one too many strange looks while emerging from an office bathroom stall—even hand-operated breast pumps make some disturbing sounds. I learned that you can tuck a baby bottle in a briefcase and still have room for your files. I cut my hair. Photos of my daughter, Amanda, at her first Independence Day party show her being held in hands still boasting my trademark long red fingernails. I made it a goal not to suddenly mutate into Betty Crocker once a baby entered the picture. I was still me, just with a new layer. I considered that a pretty nifty accomplishment.

So who'd have thought I'd decide to stay home? As we awaited the birth of our second child, God decided to relentlessly call me to something different. To stay at home.

I buckled up my courage and quit work. Sounds easy when you put in it one sentence like that, doesn't it? You and I both know that is *so* far from true, and you'll hear much more about that later.

The transformation—or perhaps lack of it—caught me totally by surprise. When I first came home, I somehow expected my DNA, the free time (Free time?!? Ha! Talk about delusions of grandeur. . .), or simply my gender to transform me into the MOM of my dreams. Well, yes, I was a mom

> This was not a retirement at all. This was a career change.

already, but staying at home full-time felt like "MOM" rather than "mom." Industrial-strength, professional-quality MOM.

Coming home doesn't work that way. As a matter of fact, for me it hardly worked at all. At-home motherhood was unexpectedly difficult. Unnervingly difficult. The magic transformation I'd expected failed to appear. Before long, I felt like I was in foreign territory and not doing well at adapting. I wasn't used to fumbling my way through things. I was the "can do" professional, the kind of person who enjoyed change and new challenges.

So why couldn't I do this?

One day I realized I wasn't succeeding in this new life because I was doing it by default. It dawned on me that I'd gone wrong in thinking of this as "a retirement" from the working world. This was not a retirement at all. This was a career change.

A career change. Aha! I had to look at this in the same way I would look at a new job. Grab this bull by the horns, attack it with the zeal that made me successful back at the office, and *learn* to be an at-home mom. Rechannel my energy and approach at home mother-hood *like the important job it is.*

This is a career. A profession. Why wasn't I treating it like one?

No one thinks twice about obtaining the necessary skills, resources, and benefits for any paid employment. Why not motherhood? Who would become a nurse or a teacher without training? Even the most dedicated workaholic executives go home at the end of the day. Librarians get sick days. Doctors take time to learn better medicine skills. Shouldn't I, as a professional mother, take my job just as seriously?

> Enter the Chief Home Officer. The lady in charge, with a vision in her head and the resources to strive for excellence.

I was onto something. There is an old saying that goes "The first part of intelligence is knowing what you're dumb at." If I was going to make a career switch into the profession of motherhood, I was wildly inexperienced. What I needed was full-scale, all-out management training.

Management Training? You bet! Mothers are, in essence, Chief Executive Officers. We run things. We manage not only households, but also the world's most intensive employee development program. So we would be smart to think of ourselves as the executives of our households.

Enter the Chief Home Officer. The lady in charge, with a vision in her head and the resources to strive for excellence.

Ladies, consider yourself officially promoted. We are the executives of our households—the Chief Home Officer. Shake off that chenille bathrobe stereotype and stand a little taller. You are a leader. A VIP.

A Big Deal

Okay, you're saying, so now instead of just a mom at home, I'm a Chief Home Officer. Big deal.

Well, it is a *very* big deal.

It might be messy, but this is still a fascinating job and a fulfilling, life-impacting career. Your work is no less than raising the next generation of the human race. Think about it—you may be raising the man or woman who will decide whether or not to launch a nuclear weapon. Or write music that will help millions make it through a hard and lonely night. Or write the defining novel of this century. Or win thousands of souls to Christ. Or become a great mom in her own right. Or be known as the best, most caring, most loyal friend to have. You are God's partner in shaping destiny one child at a time.

I hear you groaning out there. Any of us who has decided to stay home already *knows* this. It's why we came home in the first place. The words might look pretty embroidered on some cute little pillow, but they're sure not going to help get the laundry done. What mothers need is the *practical application* of our value.

How do we get from knowing our *profession* to excelling in our *professionalism*? In the following chapters I will pass on how I—and other moms like me—*learned* to thrive in at-home motherhood.

Come along on this journey with me. With a little creativity, self-awareness, and just plain guts, we can all make our work environments a lot better. Then we, in the process, become better moms.

Personal Reflections

1. THINK about your own memories of being mothered. Are they good? Negative? Nonexistent? Take some time to examine how your childhood picture of motherhood effects how you view mothering

now. Are there strengths you can draw from? Are there negatives that spark an instant, strong reaction? What are the differences between your mother and yourself? The similarities?

2. WHAT things drew you to stay at home? Do you think they are realistic or idealized? Take a moment to reflect on what you want to achieve by staying at home—both for you and your children. What have you sought to avoid or solve—for you or your children—by coming home?

3. WHICH of your character traits do you feel will help you in your new career at home? What traits might prove obstacles? This might also be a good question to ask your spouse and a close trusted friend. Take some time to reflect—in writing if you can—on what your hopes and fears for yourself are in this season of your life.

chapter 2

Management Training: Downshifting in Culture Shock

HANDS DOWN, THIS is a traumatic, wonderful, scary, life-altering job change.

Deciding to give up your career and stay home to raise your children is much like the highly personal decision to have children in the first place: it's not right until it is the right time in *your* life. And I don't believe you should do it because everyone around you seems to be doing it. When it *is* the right time, there is nothing you want more. However, that hardly makes it easy.

In my work situation, I needed to announce—rather far in advance—that I was leaving. I knew I could not hold up the pretense that I was just taking a maternity leave, that I would be coming back to my job when I knew very well that I wasn't. Yes, there were consequences in paid leave and benefits, but I couldn't knowingly deceive my employer in order to get them. I needed to do this with my head held up, with honor and integrity. I was leaving to stay home and raise my children and everyone was going to know it. It was a matter of principle to me.

This did not make announcing my plans any easier. I didn't know how it would be accepted, what people would think of my decision, or how it would affect my remaining months (yes, I gave *three months* notice ...) at work. Truth be told, I was just plain scared to "go public" with my new life goals.

Perhaps knowing my skittishness, God forced my hand. Rather soon after I had made my decision, my boss called me into an important meeting. A meeting that would be impossible to have without disclosing my plans to leave. I prepared. I prayed. I squirmed. I ate a lot of chocolate. I made sure it was scheduled for later in the day and made plans for my husband, Jeff, and daughter, Amanda, to meet me for dinner after work. If this was going to be an ugly meeting, I wanted at least some cheesecake to look forward to once it was over.

God is amazing.

That dreaded meeting has become one of the high points of my tenure at that organization. Talking about departmental plans, by boss grew uncomfortable when she told me, "I want you to do as objective an analysis as possible, but I feel uneasy because I may be asking you to evaluate yourself out of a job."

I smiled, a gush of gratitude for God's sovereignty washing over me. "That may be less of a problem than you think. Believe it or not, I will be in an exceptionally good position to give you an objective analysis."

She looked at me quizzically. Her quizzical look changed to utter surprise when I told her I would be leaving not just this organization, but work all together when the baby came. "Allie, that is the last thing I ever expected to hear from *you*. I think it's terrific, but I really never thought *you*...." And so on. She was tremendously supportive, and we both agreed it was not only a good thing for me, but a great opportunity for the organization as well. I floated out of that meeting. I sailed into dinner with an affirmation that could have only come from On High. (I still had the cheesecake.)

That was the last thing that went "better than expected" for quite a while.

On March 23, 1996, I piled the last of my files into the back of my minivan and left my working life. It certainly felt like the end of an era as I turned in my office keys and said goodbye. I had jumped like God had asked me to, made this extraordinary leap of faith into a new unknown life. But as far as I was concerned, I was still falling and no one had caught me yet. I spent that night curled up in a ball on the couch watching television—pregnancy notwithstanding, I felt drained and ill. It felt like I had just cut off a limb—a very useful, visible, attractive limb. I was unsure of what would grow back—or if anything was going to grow back at all.

This is not just a career choice, it's a transformation. Right down to the cellular level, in my opinion. In my case, it was drastic. To make such a transformation, God seemed to know that it was essential for all of the old me to be stripped away. I needed a new, clean slate with which to begin my new life.

And so, he stripped.

I mean *stripped*.

Little Boy Blue

My son's entry into the world was a two-beat drama. First, there were cheers and elation at having delivered a boy (our wish) and without a C-section (which is how I delivered Amanda). That joy was followed immediately by frantic activity and quickly mounting concern. When Christopher finally emerged, there was no lusty cry. I remember only a weak, gurgling sound. A wall of staff blocked my view as our baby was hoisted onto the medical table. The talking began to grow louder and more people entered the room. I recall only one brief glimpse of his tiny bottom. A *very blue* bottom. Then a nurse said as kindly as she could, "He's not breathing well. We're going to need to take him."

No time for the miracle of birth here, we went straight into the high drama of neonatal intensive care.

It was three hours before we knew Christopher would survive. It was probably the most fearsome crisis that had beset Jeff and me in our entire marriage. We both knew we could be looking at just one scary night, years of hardship, or even an unthinkable tragedy. It was a time for fear.

This is perhaps the only time in my life where I can say, with certainty, that I have experienced the "peace that passes all understanding" God promises us in Philippians 4:7. That supernatural peace, as it descended on me in that hospital room, is the true miracle of Christopher's birth. Our magic moments didn't come as we held our child for the first time. They came as we contemplated the very real possibility of his death or disability.

That inexplicable peace settled over me and I was filled with the assurance that we could handle whatever happened next. "We'll deal with it," I said, although I don't think either of us could look the other in the eye at that point. "No matter what happens, we'll handle it."

Eventually, everything turned out fine. The miracles and scares of those three hours, however, will remain with me for the rest of my life.

I'd like to tell you that it was all warm fuzzy newborn euphoria after that. It would make for a happy story. This still is a happy story, but we were far from out of the woods when Christopher decided he would stick around this wide, wonderful earth. He did so with a vengeance. Having scared us sufficiently with what I now call "his death-defying birth," Christopher decided to implement the H-bomb of the newborn arsenal: colic.

No, not just colic. COLIC. Red-faced, ear-piercing, sanity-withering, sleep-defying COLIC. Once he figured out this breathing stuff, it seemed the next logical step for Christopher was screaming.

Was that enough to get me out of my "I'm going to master this" mode and into "I need you Lord" mode? Evidently not.

But Wait, There's More. . .

Fast forward to O'Hare Airport, two weeks later. As we stood in line to put my mother on her plane back home, she silently slumped against me and fell to the floor unconscious. She'd been looking and feeling bad all week and we both knew something was wrong. She had even moved to an earlier flight so she could see her own doctor in Connecticut. In a span of thirty seconds my topsy-turvy world spun even further out of control. Here I was, working on three hours sleep—if even that much—my delivery stitches still stung, and I was holding my unconscious mother in my arms with a newborn in a stroller two feet away. That, ladies and gentlemen, is *stripped*. I was incapable of a cognizant thought. I didn't even have enough wits about me to get scared.

"Your mother's had a mild heart attack."

I didn't hear the "mild" part. I only heard the subsequent words like "emergency surgery now" and "intensive care." To comprehend the intensity of this moment you need to know that my father died of heart disease nearly fifteen years earlier.

The peace that enveloped me in Christopher's delivery room did not accompany me to the cardiac intensive care. That day, clinging to the pay phone in that waiting room as I made call after emergency call, seemed one of the lowest moments of my life. I was exhausted beyond clear thought. Indeed, my mind could only hold one concept: The situation I now faced was *absolutely* beyond my capacity to cope. I buckled under the emotional strain of Mom's recuperation that would now take place in my living room. I stood leaning into the hospital pay phone whimpering to my pastor's office. "Call the deacons," I wailed, too dismayed to be proud. "I don't know what kind of help I need yet, but I know I'm going to need it. I don't know how I'm going to get through this." There, in that broken moment, I let it all go and threw myself and my family at the mercy of God. I abandoned any pretense of holding it together.

It was a turning point. That desperation, which allowed me to freely accept help, was a gift in crisis clothing. I allowed myself to feel bolstered by the armies of prayer I knew had been called forth on my behalf. I stopped saying "fine" when people asked how I was. I gave myself permission to merely survive instead of manage and conquer. These were tremendous gifts I had never accepted before. They have forever changed the way I view my life. They have allowed me to live with my blunders as I have learned this new profession. Those dark moments planted the seeds of generosity and compassion. They allowed me to scratch under the shiny, glossy appearance of life and muck around in the messy truth of real life.

> *I gave myself permission to merely survive instead of manage and conquer.*

When I am really honest with myself, I spent a lot of time focusing on appearance and others' perceptions before those trying days. Now, I'd like to think I concern myself much more with what is authentic. As far as I can tell, it is not a switch that could have been made without a drastic set of circumstances.

Christopher's colic had little regard for Mom's recovery, Amanda's adjustment, or any of the other pressing concerns in my life. I made do with four or five hours of sleep a night. I, who had worried how I would fill my days, was now just trying to survive them. I, who had wondered how much I would miss my work, couldn't even think as far as the next meal. The woman who used to wonder if her nail polish was chipped now merely hoped she had both socks on. The "take charge" lady now relied on her Lord for each hour and the will to drag her feet out of bed at 1 A.M. to rock a screaming, red-faced infant for hours.

I look back—now—with the unshakable knowledge that *I* did not get myself through this. *God* picked me up and carried me, just like in the familiar "Footprints" story.

And I know that the ability to *lean so completely on one's God* is an extraordinary blessing. The unshakable knowledge that he pulled me through has given me the strength—or rather the recognition of his strength—to face the challenges of motherhood. I don't tell you these stories to evoke pity or to dramatize my life. I tell you of my heart-rending transition into motherhood so you'll understand the source of my strength. So you will know that no matter how God chooses to strip you—or has already stripped you—it serves a purpose.

> No matter how God chooses to strip you— or has already stripped you—it serves a purpose.

I needed industrial-strength stripping because at-home motherhood, for me, represented an industrial-strength transition. The Bible is filled with people who received extensive overhauls—Moses, David, Paul, just to name a few—to prepare them for God's plans. Why should we, as co-crafters of little souls, not have the same experience?

As such, while it was an excruciating one, I would not trade the month of April 1996 for anything. Unless, of course, someone found an easier way to build that kind of holy reliance. But I don't think it works that way.

The Daily Domestic Blues

By mid-May, Mom was 110 percent recuperated and on her way home. All crises had subsided and I was left with the less sensational task of crafting a new domestic existence. While Christopher's colic didn't go away for another two months, we did manage to rid him of his hideous custom of screaming from 1–5 A.M. Now he screamed from 1–5 P.M., which was still no fun but a lot more manageable.

I expected our new way of life to be an adjustment for me, but I was unprepared for how difficult leaving day care would be for Amanda. Everything I looked at—friends' advice, books, magazines—focused on my adjustment. No one mentioned how to adapt *children* to coming home. I guess we all assumed she'd be just plain thrilled to have Mom home all day with her and that would be the end of it. I mean really, Mom at home is the ideal option, right? What every child truly desires? Who would think you need coping skills for *that*?

In all truth, we had asked a great deal of this poor little four-year-old in facing the chaos of April. I was raw from all the strain, just beginning to heal as the summer set in. When people would ask Amanda what she thought of her little brother, she would reply wearily, "He cries a lot." I am sometimes amazed she adapted as well as she did. It was, however, a bumpy ride.

There are scads of books and magazine articles giving advice on preparing a child to welcome (I use that word loosely) a new sibling into the family. None of those helpful resources prepared me for Amanda's tremendous adjustment of going from day care to staying home. At day care, Amanda had playmates all day, lots of cool toys, kid-focused food, fieldtrips, and Dixie cups with riddles on them. At home, she had Mom (who wasn't good at Barbies and too tired to play tag) and a screaming, wet, smelly, Mommy-attention-sapping lump called Christopher.

I was shocked to realize that after four years as a parent I neither knew how to play, nor liked it, nor was I any good at it. After about fifteen minutes, Legos and dollhouses were boring to me. Don't get me wrong, it's not that I ignored my daughter as a working mom, but for some reason I can't explain, playing nights and weekends isn't anything like full-time mommy-style playing. Endlessly reenacting the same illogical sequence of Barbie events, whose importance was known only to Amanda, is trying. How many times can you read *One Fish Two Fish Red Fish Blue Fish* before your eyes glaze over in rhyming dementia? The endless choruses of "Mommy, watch me!" The eight-second attention span. You know being with her, sharing her world with her is important, but the sheer repetition of it all can drive you to your breaking point.

It's the repetition that makes it so hard to do full time. You can sing the same silly song for about an hour. You can put up with tantrums for about an hour. But string them all together in an eight-hour day and you've got a recipe for disastrous impatience. Add the emotional/physical strain of a new baby in the house, and things go from bad to worse. Amanda was used to constant child companionship. We were blessed with quality day care and she very much enjoyed her days there. Now I was the sole playmate. It was exhausting. It was exasperating. Everybody was unhappy.

Things simply could not go on as they were. Adopting my usual business strategy, I spent some time identifying the problem. As far as I could tell, we were bored. It wasn't realistic to expect us to downshift into at-home speed in the span of four weeks, no matter how much Christopher had commandeered our lives. I have talked with several other newly-at-home moms who say they experienced the same culture shock. Everything is slower when you're at home full time—that's both a good and a bad thing. Everything slows down even further when a baby enters the picture. Remember when you could grab your purse and run to the store? Leave the house at 7:20 for a 7:30 movie? Doesn't the thought of that make you *salivate* these days?

> *Going from a job to being at home, from woman to parent, is culture shock no matter how you slice it.*

This issue attacks not just women who decided to no longer be working moms, but new moms who have known all along that they would stay home once they had children. Going from a job to being at home, from woman to parent, is culture shock no matter how you slice it.

Hugging The Learning Curve

I elected to attack the problem by starting from where we were and working to where we wanted to be. Amanda and I were used to full, busy days full of busy people, so I set about to schedule us into an active family life that mimicked our working days. We would do the "9 to 5" thing, just not at the office and at a more baby-friendly speed. It sounds odd now, but it was a much-needed coping strategy when we were just learning this at-home stuff. A learning curve, if you will.

I set two ground rules. Rule one was that everyone was dressed (and for me that included hair, make-up, and no sweats!) by 10 A.M. This gave me permission to put Christopher, who had now gained the nickname "CJ," in his crib for fifteen minutes, even if he was crying, and take care of myself. I'm just not the kind of person who can spend the day in her pajamas and feel good about the world. Not to mention that the simple act of taking a shower became a ten-minute vacation. You can't hear a baby cry in the shower.

Rule two was that unless there was a compelling reason to stay home (and some days there were dozens of those), we went out somewhere every morning and most afternoons. In short, we forcibly reinjected ourselves into the human race. We got a zoo membership—worth its weight in gold for young families. Pool passes were such a blessing—afternoon fussy time became (and we actually called it this) "Fussing By The Pool" and it was somehow much easier to endure. We signed up for library story hours, made an event out of walking to the corner for ice cream, and learned the fine art of visiting the mall for no real reason except a cinnamon bun (ooh, but you have to be careful with this one). I scoured the paper for anything even remotely interesting to do. Story hour at the local coffeeshop/bookstore. The neighborhood farmer's market. Any park that had different equipment than the one close to home. Duck feeding. Museums, large and small. Department store promotions. Every park district's free anything for miles around. I broke my weekly grocery shopping into smaller biweekly trips. I have since learned how to stay home all day and even enjoy it, but back then it was inconceivable and probably dangerous.

Adventures in Networking

Even the busiest trio can only entertain themselves for so long—especially if one of them is an infant. We needed company, and lots of it. I made a list of Amanda's friends from church and preschool and began to schedule two playdates a week. I invited the moms to stay for lunch so I would have a shot at participating in adult conversation and receiving advice. Several moms, a few of whom have become dear friends, humored my all-too-numerous requests for visits and held my hand during those scary first months. A few endured some pretty odd behavior as I groped my way around in this new role.

One mom got a healthy dose of my loose grip on mom-reality. Mustering my courage to join the tight circle of moms picking up their daughters from preschool, I asked if she and her children would like to join us for lunch on a particular day. She looked at me oddly, for I had chosen a date *two weeks* in the future. *Two weeks!* It makes me cringe to think of it now. "I don't even know what I'm doing this afternoon!" the woman replied in a baffled but amused voice. I flipped open my computerized date-book—can you imagine? But, God love her, she accepted anyway.

I was excited. I'd made a playdate. I was on my way. I was a Networking Mom.

Two weeks later, I set the table.

No, I SET THE TABLE.

I set it the way you would if you asked an *adult* over to lunch. China—okay, the everyday stuff but still nothing plastic—cloth napkins, glassware, not one but *two* forks (one for salad, you know). I served pumpkin soup, biscuits, and pasta salad.

What was I thinking?

Does any child under the age of twenty-seven deign to eat pumpkin soup? It's a *vegetable,* for heaven's sake. Not a speck of peanut butter in sight. And nothing, nothing on the table was shaped like any character seen on television. I can't even begin to imagine what this poor mom thought as she entered our dining room—*our dining room!* Some sort of Martha Stewart-esque nightmare.

It was a full six months before the idiocy of what I had done struck me like a ton of Lennox. Although we met for lunch several times and our daughters played frequently, it was always at a restaurant and never at her house. Gee, imagine that. Would *you* invite me over to lunch after that fiasco?

The Department of Motherhood Personnel

I can think of dozens of huge, gaping errors that I made as a newly at-home mom. I can also name dozens of king-sized mistakes I made in my first few years in the working world. It's not that different. New is new, no matter what the circumstances.

New jobs are just that: new jobs. It's the role of the manager and human resources to give wet-behind-the-ears recruits the tools, training, and resources they need to learn the job. They get Management Training. All that stuff—including that thing you once had called a paycheck—fall under what's called a compensation package.

You've been plunked squarely down in the role of Chief Home Officer. No matter how many days old that shirt is you've got on, you are an executive woman. But you can't use your old version of the term "executive." The world's view of an "executive" is the woman who gets all the perks. The one with the hefty compensation package that includes an armload of benefits.

We need to shift our thinking. Let's take this executive package and turn it on its ear. Let's take a look at the compensation package for the Chief Home Officer.

The trouble is, you won't find a human resources department to lay it out nicely for you. I couldn't even find a Department of Motherhood Personnel (I figured I'd better know where that was so I'd know where to run to resign).

Actually, I did find the Department of Motherhood Personnel: it's me.

That means it is *my* responsibility now to make sure I have the tools, training, and resources I need to learn this new job. Consequently, I have set my mind to my own training and have been surprised with the results. I've made myself a rather attractive little benefits package for this career of mine. You can too.

Maybe you have been an executive or an entrepreneur, and you understand how to find resources you need to reach a goal, but never thought of it in terms of your motherhood. Maybe you have been an accountant, a store clerk, or a cook, and that kind of entrepreneurial thinking is as foreign to you as the formula for amoxicillin. It doesn't matter—we are all on the bottom of the learning curve here. It's time to start climbing. You will be amazed at what's out there for you if you get creative and determined. It's time to begin tapping into those benefits.

Personal Reflections

1. Did the way you left your working life make your transition to full-time motherhood easier or more difficult? Do you have regrets about how you left? What fears were realized? What fears did you discover you did not need to have?

2. READ Philippians 4. Can you think of a time where the "peace that passes all understanding" has come in your life? What did you learn from that experience?

3. HAS there been a time in your life when you thought you were beyond your ability to cope? Do you feel like you are there now? What ways can you keep yourself grounded during such a time? What makes things worse?

4. WHERE in your life do you lean on God? Where do you fail to lean on him, relying on your own strength instead? What happens in each of those instances? Where do you sense God is calling you to lean on him these days? What's keeping you from doing so?

chapter 3

CHO Employee Benefit #1: Paychecks

IT'S NOT HARD to know where to start in the Chief Home Officer compensation package: The heart of every benefits package always includes the paycheck. We care a lot about paychecks. Today's society does a lethal job of anchoring your self-esteem to the size of your paycheck. As stay-at-home moms, we no longer have that measuring stick. When you remove that system of valuation, something new has to take its place. Something other than money.

Yet, we can't wipe money from the picture entirely, either. More than likely, money figures rather prominently in your daily life now because you have to be more careful with it. As a stay-at-home mom, your job now is not to earn the money, but to devote time and energy to see that it is spent as wisely and as efficiently as possible. Stretching that dollar, you will discover if you haven't already, is a mighty big job.

Yes, I have become the bargain-hunter I'd never thought I'd be. If you are one of those women with the extraordinary gift for locating a great deal, you're already one up on the game. Cutting costs are skills we all can learn in this season at home—and they're skills that will have a lasting impact on the rest of your life. Trust me, if you ever bought yourself an $80 pair of shoes during your working life—even as a splurge—you may never be able to stomach it again. ("That's a good thing!" husbands across America are saying. Hmm, now let's talk about power tools and car accessories, gentlemen...)

In all our new attention to the bottom line, however, let's remember that wisely doesn't *always* mean cheaply. Some things that may seem frivolous at first are actually wise investments.

"I don't get a paycheck, I'm a stay-at-home mom now!" you say.

I say think again. How you deal with money is integral to your success as a mother.

Jeff and I were the quintessential, equality-laden '90s couple. We had "his," "hers," and "ours" checkbooks. Jeff

> How you deal with money is integral to your success as a mother.

and I spend money as differently as black and white. He saves and saves for big purchases. I love to nickel and dime life. I'm thrilled with a bottle of nail polish, or most of all, a double-mocha latte. Jeff loves to research, to compare quality, to consider options. I am the ultimate impulse buyer. These styles don't get along well in the same checkbook. While we never had marital tension about the basic operational costs of life, we found things worked much more smoothly when we kept our discretionary income separate. It was actually four years into our marriage before we had a joint credit card.

Effective as it was, this system was useless in a single-income situation. It was one of the most basic, yet challenging, adaptations we had to make once I came home. Money is one of those things that rarely contains itself to it's own single issue. Emotions, values, life goals, and all kinds of secondary issues come creeping around the corner once you start messing with the money side of things.

Baby equipment has a tremendous talent for unearthing this issue. Every item contains a value decision: Do we buy the very best for our precious little one? Or do we spend sparingly, knowing that items get outgrown quickly? Must our child have new things in the very best condition with no chance of germs or defect, or are we comfortable with the idea of something another child has used—and perhaps loved? Don't even start with cloth versus disposable diapers—that's a marriage-strainer all on it's own.

The impulse to spoil runs rampant. The tight checkbook exerts a deadly squeeze. Whew! This hot potato requires hefty doses of sensitivity and creative thinking.

The solution looks different for every family. You may find your financial behavior is very close to that of your husband's. Or, like us, you'll come to realize (if you haven't already) just how different you are. As I said, if you've furnished a nursery by now, you've hit up against some of these thorny issues. It's important to carefully consider what's going to meet the needs of your family.

Jeff and I, while shopping for Amanda's baby equipment, were prime marketing fodder. Amanda was our first child, and we were thrilled to be becoming parents. We made two rather telling purchases for her: a stroller and a mattress.

Amanda's stroller was one of those top of the line, Italian models. The sportscar of strollers (now, it seems, they also come in SUV versions). Stylish. Matching pads for this and that. Classy. Full of options. In hindsight, it might have been a bit extreme, but it was an important piece of equipment. One that would get daily use. And I saw it, in some ways, as much a personal expression of our style as the car one drives.

Can you say that of a crib mattress? One savvy sales lady had us convinced our purchase of a crib mattress was as crucial as Amanda's choice of college. She must have seen our naive excitement coming a mile off. She reminded us how Amanda's little bones would be developing as she slept on it, how lack of support might damage her delicate stature, how most people overlook this crucial detail. Man, we were hooked!

We came close to spending a huge amount of money on that crib mattress. Then we got home and the hypnotism wore off. A mattress. Think about all the places babies sleep, all the odd angles they curl themselves into, and you realize the mattress has almost nothing to do with it. Heck, Amanda's favorite place to sleep was a thirty-year-old wicker bassinet with a bath towel folded up inside of it.

But don't you see how the visibility of the stroller, it's reflection as an accessory of our new life, impacted our decision? In the end, it wasn't a totally bad choice—that stroller held up to some mighty tough abuse. But we didn't need the import model. I'm guessing a run of the mill stroller might have fared just as well. The comparison of these two items, however, makes a neat little microcosm of our financial adaptations as parents.

The Power of Pocketmoney

We had to change the way we did business as a family. Adapt from our former two-income ways. After much pondering, I devised a system that applied much of our original concepts to a single-income budget. The cliff-jumping step of ditching the triple-checkbook system and putting everything into one joint account was a tough one. Primarily for Jeff. Trusting me not to empty the checkbook on hormone-induced impulse buys took no small amount of faith on his part.

At the beginning of the year, Jeff and I discussed what were his major purchase plans for the next twelve months. He always knew that kind of stuff in advance so it was ready information. We grafted those expenses (moderated for a single income, of course) into our household budget. Then we added another crucial line designed to meet my needs: "Allie's pocket money." I looked at all the places where I draw fun from my spending and came up with a weekly amount that would let me do just enough of that to feel good. Not all of it, just enough. Little things like a lunch out now and then, an item or two of clothing a month, a few magazines, and the requisite latte. For some women it may be $5 a week, others may be able to afford as much as $30 a week. It depends on your budget and what makes you smile. Sometimes all it takes is a $2 magazine and a hot bath with no interruptions. Other days. . .

The important thing is that those purchases were mine to make without any necessary forethought or approval. I had the opportunity to do the impulse buying that gave me a bit of fun in my life. If I wanted to blow a month's worth of pocket money in one frivolous impulse purchase, that was my choice. Or, I could judiciously dole it out to myself over the month with little goodies each week.

It may seem like a little thing or you may only have a small amount of money to do this, but I have no doubt that this purchasing power played a large role in maintaining my self-esteem, happiness, and even sanity in those months of adjustment. It is recognizing that we have come from a working world that centers—like it or not—in monetary value and that we need to take steps to ease the transition.

More than that, however, this strategy recognizes the emotional strain of our new job. It fosters my ability to take the steps that will keep my spirits as strong as my antiseptic wipes. The deliberate act of giving myself a line item in our family budget that was purely for my personal enjoyment validated my worth in this family. A financial expression that my happiness mattered. Many of my friends who made the transition from work to

> Many of my friends who made the transition from work to home tell me of missing bringing home a paycheck and the worth they felt it gave them.

home tell me of missing bringing home a paycheck and the worth they felt it gave them. I never mourned the loss of my breadwinner status because our family budgeting process affirmed my worth.

Money is tight when you cut off one income and you have to be extra careful. Don't do it, though, at the expense of your own empowerment—you are managing a family now. Sometimes you know best of all what needs to be bought. I would be shopping with friends and they would remark that they ought to discuss it with their husbands before purchasing even a small such-and-such. I never needed a moment's hesitation if it wasn't a major purchase (those were always, by agreement and at a specified dollar level, discussed first). If it was within my line item, I bought it. If it was something for the house or the kids, I knew what our budget was and if we could make the purchase. I was a family manager with an expense account, not a housewife waiting for her weekly allowance from Hubby's paycheck. Such affirmation made all the difference in the world.

There was another unexpected side effect from this system. I cashed this paycheck in front of my children. Yes, I felt silly when one day we pulled up to the bank drive-thru and my two-year-old son yelled "cheeseburger" into the window, confusing it with You-Know-Where. I discovered, however, that my children admired my monthly paycheck. It was like a great big, grown-up allowance to them. I suppose that's not far from the truth, but when I explained that it was for the things Mommy likes to do and little fun things for all of us during the month, I believe they began to understand that well-being is important. That money is really just a tool, not an end in itself. And, hopefully, that Mommy's job is just as important as Daddy's job.

Money *is* a tool. Like all good tools, it matters greatly how you wield it. All of us have known parents or grandparents from the Depression Era who make themselves crazy saving a little money here, a little money there, putting themselves through tremendous inconvenience and hardship all the while. How often do we eventually discover that this person actually had more than enough money to live comfortably? That despite an abundance of resources, they could never escape a mindset of scarcity?

A Clean Getaway

I believe newly at-home mothers face the same dangers of scarcity-based thinking. Terrified about the consequences of one-income living, we can take an ax to some expenses that are actually unwise to cut from the budget. One of these emotionally-charged items for me was babysitting. Not babysitting for Jeff and I to go out on a "date"—those funds came from another pool—but sitting for me to get away from the kids during daytime hours.

My brain kept classifying this as a "luxury." Then I slowly began to realize the immense recuperative powers of time away. I could schedule a lunch with a friend, keep up with some former colleagues, or just go sit in the coffee shop and remember what silence feels like. It doesn't have to be a huge expense. Moms with tight finances can take advantage of park district "Mom's Day Out" programs, co-ops, or trade sitting. This is one of those areas, however, where you have to act like a manager and be proactive. You have to think ahead, recognize the issue, and cope with it before you are entangled in the consequences. In short, you have to go get it—it won't come to you.

> My brain kept classifying this as a "luxury." Then I slowly began to realize the immense recuperative powers of time away.

Some weeks I didn't need a break. Others I needed every minute I could carve away from those children. *And that does not make me a bad mother.* Sometimes all I needed was just knowing the escape clause was there.

My sanity, my personhood other than motherhood, was worth the investment. For motherhood is a job, and no one can be productive if they don't get away from their job regularly.

The problem is, you don't leave motherhood at 5 P.M. You can't help but bring your work home with you because it's right there, clinging to your shins while you're trying to make dinner. As an at-home mother, you have to make your own breaks. Failing to do so, I strongly believe, lessens your own self-esteem, your happiness in your career, and ultimately the impact you can have on your children. A wiped-out, burned-out, stressed-out woman is the worst example of motherhood you can show your children. If you do not feel good about what you do (okay, 80 percent of the time), your children will pick up on it fast and decide that being with them isn't fun. We have all felt what it's like to be tolerated rather than enjoyed. That is not a message I want to send to my kids.

In addition, I feel it is vital for my children to learn that taking care of myself is important. Self-care is an essential element in the successful adult. Identifying your own needs and finding ways to meet them are crucial life skills. Any glance at the headlines will tell you they are skills greatly lacking these days. Heart attacks, depression, high blood pressure, obesity—we comprise a society bathed in self-centeredness but sadly lacking in self-care. God tells us to love our neighbor *as* ourselves. More than any stroll down the bulging Self Help aisle of any bookstore, I believe my children learn most by *watching me loving and honoring me in addition to loving and honoring them*. My body and spirit are the tools of my trade. Creativity, optimism, and perspective rarely come in "just add water and mix" formulas (lattes and hot fudge not withstanding). Perhaps the most potent truth of all is that I cannot give to my children emotional resources I do not have myself.

> I cannot give to my children emotional resources I do not have myself.

I have learned the hard way: This time to myself is no luxury—it is as essential as sleep and food. If I skip it for a few weeks, I watch my patience wear thin and I snap at my kids. Young children have a high annoyance factor. Every day takes a constant squelching of the urge to get mad or frustrated. The repetition. The objections to even the simplest of requests. The unmerciful, unending wails of a sick or cranky baby. It is so easy to snap. Let's add a potent collection of hormones to the mix and you've got a recipe for disaster. I have a theatrically trained voice than can spit venom when I'm angry. When I snap, I really snap. I snarl. I don't like my children to hear it if I can help it. My time to myself—and the affirmation investing in it brings—is my best weapon against snapping. It gives me the bottomless pit of patience and love it takes to raise small children full-time.

The Chief Home Officer paycheck doesn't look like the one many of us used to bring home. It can, however, serve many of the same purposes. Look past the dollar signs to what that income *brought* you as a person, rather than what it *bought* you, and you're on the right track to building your own CHO paycheck.

Personal Reflections

1. IN what ways do you grieve the loss of your paycheck and breadwinning status? Look past the dollars (or new lack of them) and think about how your job effected your self-esteem. What's gone now? Are there voids or are new things taking their place?

2. EXAMINE your parents' relationship to money. How does it effect you? Do you think of yourself as a person of abundance or scarcity? How does that affect financial decisions you make—large and small?

3. CRAFT yourself A paycheck. Make a list of ten things that make you happy and how much each costs. Pick two or three smaller items. Can you find that much in your weekly budget? If you think you can't, try it for one week and see what happens. You may find it is more important than other things you thought you needed.

CHO Employee Benefit #2: Time Off

THE REST OF the working world gets to go home at 5 P.M. (or thereabouts).

We don't.

Yes, I know our commute has now become nonexistent, and that's part of the attraction. But we overlook the cost. Motherhood is the *original* 24/7/365. Sounds rather simple, but this took me quite a while to recognize. It is one of the basic truths and tortures of at-home motherhood. We are very good at forgetting the negative power of repeated, prolonged exposure. The stuff of Chinese water torture. Until I figured out a mother's lack of time off, I couldn't understand why I was so tired all the time.

No, tired is what comes from not having enough sleep—and mothers know the definition of *that* all too well. I was *weary*.

Managing a house is cyclical, repetitive work. Most of the time it is blatantly void of tangible accomplishments. To me it felt like I was living in the twenty-first century version of the myth of Sisyphus. Sisyphus's eternal punishment (as in *not* a choice gig) was to spend all day pushing an enormous boulder up a hill, only to watch it roll back down at the end of the day. Then he would get up the next day and push it back up the hill all over again. Sound like the very definition of futility? Sound familiar? You load the dishwasher only to unload it an hour later—and put more dishes in that will have to be unloaded later. You take the laundry out of the dryer only to put more in. Endless cycles of diaper changes. You can spend four hours cleaning your house, and I guarantee your toddlers can trash it in four minutes.

Few jobs in the working world deal with that level of futility. And all of them don't extend much past a forty-hour work week. Jeff would come home from work and change gears along with his tie and shoes. Not so with motherhood. At 5 P.M. I would still have dinner, dishes, baths, and the couple of loads of laundry that didn't get finished that morning because somebody wanted to finger paint.

By the third month it began to wear me down. I would curse inwardly at 9 P.M. as I dragged the hamper up the stairs from the laundry room for the umpteenth time that day while Jeff sat reading. In his defense, he had worked all day and deserved his rest. I could not begrudge him refuge from his daily toil to provide for our family. Yet, I was still bitter and frustrated. I agreed with my friend when she told me once in a strained voice, "I feel like a maintenance worker."

The Maritime Miracle

Then one day I remembered something my brother said when he returned home from a school internship on a marine research vessel. Like our house, research on this ship did not stop at 5 P.M., but went on around the clock. Workers on board this ship accomplished their tasks in four-hour shifts—four hours on, four hours off. This struck me as part of the solution to my onslaught of drudgery. My day didn't look like 9–5 anymore, yet I was expecting my rest to stay on that schedule. I would toil and toil in the expectation of evening rest, not recognizing that 5 P.M. was really the start of my second shift. No wonder I was exhausted in both body and spirit. And we all know how much patience it takes to deal with small children at dinnertime. Jeff would often come home to nasty pandemonium—not a welcome I wanted to give him and not one he enjoyed.

Perhaps this research vessel had something to teach me. Eagerly, I embraced the nautical approach and broke my days down into shifts of off and on. Gradually I came to realize that my "evening" rest came in the afternoon. I needed to find ways to give myself downtime between my two "shifts." Now I was not going to get four hours off for my four hours on, but there were ways to accomplish the same goal in a smaller amount of time. I figured even thirty minutes might be enough to do the trick.

I instituted "quiet time" for Amanda while Christopher was napping. I got creative in involving the children in the housework so I could get a good chunk of it done in the morning. Did you know most dollar stores sell small, brightly colored feather dusters? With the right promotion, it becomes a toy. I figured, any dust they actually got up was a plus. The nifty plastic dust mops with disposable pads they sell these days are made just for little people to zoom around on the living room floor. Get a mechanical carpet sweeper and play restaurant. And Holy Hoovers, Batman, who would have thought my toddler would be so fond of the vacuum cleaner (canister rides notwithstanding)?

> Gradually I came to realize that my "evening" rest came in the afternoon. I needed to find ways to give myself downtime between my two "shifts."

Hardest of all, I forcefully ignored the impulse to get a million things done while Christopher was sleeping and ordered myself onto the couch with a book or magazine. *On* the couch, as in feet up and *not* folding laundry. I asked for a cappuccino machine for Christmas so Mom could indulge in her favorite beverage during downtime (I admit a shot of caffeine at 2 P.M. helped a lot). The physical break wound its way into my mindset. As the days went by, my brain began to work in split shifts rather than in corporate workdays. Even time spent with Amanda during the early afternoon (no five year old endures "quiet time" for much more than forty-five minutes) was relegated to quieter fun such as playing tea party, coloring, or reading books. Warm, soft, togetherness nourished my spirit just as much as a nap on the couch.

No, it wasn't four hours. Some days it felt like four minutes. Most of the time, however, it was a shift in thinking that brought about extraordinary change in our home. These days I have taken it so far as to move my shower to mid-afternoon so that it truly feels like a new start (it helps with that infamous morning rush too). Before, Jeff often walked through the door in the evening to a family at wits end. Now, he usually (but not always) finds a freshened, refreshed wife with kids who are at some semblance of peace. Now that my children are old enough to do some things unsupervised, their allotted TV time comes during the late afternoon as well—it becomes downtime for everyone. The system has become so smooth that I can often squeeze in a devotional time while the kids watch their beloved *Magic School Bus*. They're happy, I'm recharged, and life is better. I can attack the evening's dinner, dishes, baths, bed—and yes—laundry with energy and sanity.

And I can be a friendly, supportive wife to my husband instead of a grimy blob who grumbles while folding laundry at the other end of the couch. Don't ever write off the value of "being there" for your spouse. It is perhaps the best reason of all to take up maritime hours in your home.

What Every Slug Knows

Time off can also mean a break for the whole family. Our family has happened on a quirky tradition known as "slug day." Slug day is the day when you suspend the rules (within reason) for everybody. It means everyone can lounge around like a slug (hence the name) on the couch in their pajamas watching TV until noon. It means lunch can be eaten in front of the television. It means we can eat pudding for breakfast. Slug day is to our family what "mental health days" are to working people. A chance to break out of the everyday for absolutely no reason at all other than for a needed break.

Mom can invoke "slug day," or any child can request a "slug day approval" from Mom. I invoke slug days when I need to take a breath or when one—and sometimes even all—of us isn't feeling up to snuff. I have invoked a slug day when I know my littlest one needs lots of cuddling. Although he was once too little to ask for a slug day, even when he was small he knew what I meant when I said "we're having a slug day." And usually, he would smile and snuggle in tighter to show his appreciation. This kind of pajama-coated cuddling reminds us of how much fun it is to just *be us*. Amanda is old enough to know when she's overwrought—most of the time. When she requests a slug day, it's a red flag to me that things have gotten out of hand and it's time to slow down. While she has certainly requested it, slug day *does not* get her out of school.

Slug day may sound silly, but I believe it teaches our children the importance of rest. Somehow the silly name helps them get their small minds around the idea. They learn that it is okay, not necessarily to break the rules, but to leave them behind for a while. To listen when their bodies say "take it easy." Like their namesakes, my little slugs learn not to be rigid, to take it slow, and to learn the fine art of what my mother called "lollygagging." As far as I'm concerned, anyone who grows up without these skills is a heart attack waiting to happen.

Often slug days engender other hidden benefits. Conversations happen that perhaps might not have happened on a tighter schedule. I learn little bits and pieces of how they view the world that only come after extended close contact. And if I am listening carefully enough, I will discover the root of a problem that has been plaguing them for some time. A large chunk of downtime with your children generally yields astounding results.

All this rest is no cure-all for the challenges of full-time motherhood. There are still days when the children are sick or just plain wild, and I am pulling my hair out and ready to run. When nerves are so frazzled a week of slug days wouldn't soothe them. I am still known to whine (hopefully out of children's earshot) "This is why some species *eat their young!*" as I thrust my offspring onto their father as he walks in the door. It happens probably more often than I realize or am ready to admit. But it happens much less often now than when I first came home. I believe it is because with scheduled rest, I have more patience and more creativity to deal with whatever comes my way each day.

My pastor pointed out this week that in the Bible the "Keep the Sabbath" commandment gets the most verbiage of any of the Ten Commandments. Evidently God knew we would need a lot of convincing. Did you ever stop to realize the high value God places on rest? "Take a day off" is right up there with "don't kill anyone." They're not as unrelated as you might think. Without rest, we do run the risk of grave consequences—not only for ourselves, but those around us.

If God, endless source of power and creator of the universe, rested on the seventh day, doesn't that speak volumes about our needs as frail human creatures? America's culture likes to pretend that the truly strong, the truly effective, don't need rest. Even our children are starved for unscheduled down time, and we are all beginning to pay the price. If you need another reason to carve out some rest for yourself, the fact that *God commanded you* should do the trick. It is not a suggestion. Your Creator knows what you need.

Diapering with a Scenic View

Now that we are all in agreement that daily rest is as essential as food and sleep, let's contend with an even bigger picture: vacations.

Vacations? Remember them? Those two weeks of glory from the working world? Luxury. Exotic locales. Fun-filled getaways. Where are they now?

There are days—warm, sunny afternoons in the park or exploring the zoo—when my life feels like the greatest of vacations. I feel so blessed to be able to spend such quality *and* quantity time with my little ones. To sidestep the daily grind of earning a living and to enjoy the constant pleasure of making a life. Of discovering how little lives are made.

Then there are days where I would give *body parts* to be sitting *alone* (okay, maybe my husband is there somewhere) in the *quiet* on a tropical island with someone *waiting on me.* These days usually happen in January following the fifteenth cold and/or flu of the school year. Or in August when it seems like it will be another millennia until the temperature comes out of the nineties and the kids go back to school.

Sure, a key to our success as mothers lies in our ability to appreciate the everyday wonders. But that can only take you so far. An important part of true rest and refreshment is time away from the everyday.

"Away from the everyday." I learned early on in my full-time-mothering career that it is not as easy as it seems. Family vacations are just that—*family* vacations. No matter how fond you are of your family, a "family vacation" is not much of a vacation when you're with family full time the other fifty weeks of the year. If you decide to spend your vacation in a cabin or visiting relatives, you may be loathe to discover that it is just transplanted everyday life for Mom. Dishes still need doing, kids still need supervising—and may need even more in someone else's home. Dressing, diapering, and baths won't take a holiday. In fact, leaving home tends to complicate things and make even more work for Mom even if Dad is around full-time to help. Anyone who has tried to get a fussy baby to sleep in a port-a-crib knows a hotel room can be a mighty tiny place. Cutting down the family income whittles down the options as well.

It is important to take time to consider what will refresh you. *Where* is an important issue, but it is the *what* of a vacation that is so crucial to its success. As I sat down to plan our first family vacation with me home full-time, God somehow gave me the wisdom to make a list of what each member of our family needed from a vacation. Jeff, who had worked a vicious schedule that year, needed relaxation and a chance to unwind. What the man really needed was to slouch in a lounge chair with a good book for about a month. Amanda, on the other hand, needed activities. Not just any activity, but new, exciting things she didn't get to do everyday. Not a heavy schedule, just a brand new one. After so much of tailoring her life to the urgent needs of others, Amanda needed a place where she could often get the chance to do just what she wanted for as long as she wanted, without having to stop because of someone else's needs or time commitment. Baby Christopher needed some structure and the chance to get a good nap in his own port-a-crib every day. What did I need? I needed a shot at some peace and quiet, no laundry, no cooking, no dishes, and no stuffing kids into car seats to get to location X by time Y. Someplace where the words "hurry up" and "we're late" would never have cause to leave my mouth for a whole week. We needed someplace where the fun didn't have to stop for everyone else if Christopher (or even Mom) needed to go home and sleep. And *no one* needed a long car ride or a stressful day at the airport.

I tend toward BIG THINGS TO DO or RELATIVES TO VISIT when I plan vacations. As I looked at my list, I became keenly aware that it was time to rethink my definition.

The vacation I discovered to meet all these needs looked nothing like my old vacations. In fact, I'd have to say it was quite the opposite. Through some church friends, I came across a tiny family resort in Michigan, about three hours from our home. We would be in a three-room cabin (translation: Mom and Dad have a different room than the kids) with a kitchenette, just a sixty-second walk from the pool and the small beach. Meals were included at the resort's main house. Two small towns were a ten-minute drive away if we needed something else to do. The place was family-oriented, so Amanda was bound to find playmates within the week's stay if not in the first thirty minutes. It was the kind of place where you could go to breakfast in your bathing suit and not change until you threw on a pair of shorts for dinner. It fit our budget and my criteria. Not exotic. Not lush. Dangerously close to boring. It was the kind of place I'd never even think of as a working woman.

> *The goal of our time away these days is to restore, reconnect, refresh, and recreate.*

It was a completely unexciting but marvelously restorative vacation. When you get right down to it, isn't that really what it's about? The time will come when traveling means ticking off another exciting place on our passports, but it won't be soon. The goal of our time away these days is to restore, reconnect, refresh, and recreate. Not to come home with cool souvenirs or breathtaking photos.

Yes, Christopher slept horribly the first few nights in our low-key, three-room hide-a-way, but both he and I could catch up on our sleep in the afternoons. Jeff got to sit around and do nothing, which he sorely needed. Mostly by the pool, because Amanda made friends instantly and was nearly waterlogged from spending so much time there. Jeff and I could sit in beach chairs and watch the kids make up silly games on the sand after dinner. Meals were family style, so if Christopher decided that all he would eat that day were pickles and croutons (one dinner's actual menu for the little guy!), it was no big deal. I got to gab with other moms around the pool. It was relaxing without being boring. It was wonderful.

Had I gone with my first instinct, however, to go somewhere museum/relative/theme park/landmark interesting, we'd have wound up exhausted. Overtaxed from demanded fun, slugging it out in a hotel, and eating meals in restaurants. I am convinced I would have come back from such a vacation fatigued and frustrated. As wonderful as Disney World sounds, it would have been more of a family project for us than a holiday. Our oldest was seven before I realized all my kids really cared about in vacations was the hotel pool. Everything else is either frosting or frustration. We would have broken our backs, our budget, and our hearts. We'll get to the Magic Kingdom someday, but right now that's not the kind of vacation we need.

Time Away As a Twosome

Family vacations, however, are not the only kind of vacation a mom needs. Someone once said, "the most important thing you can do for your children is to love their father." I believe in making the hard work of keeping a marriage a priority. And I am now a firm believer in getting away without your kids at least once a year— preferably two or three times. Yes, you heard me, two or three times.

Before you gasp, you should know I was not raised this way. My parents did not take trips without us until I was old enough to drive. I have to say, however, that they had a very good marriage. So the thought of getting away without the kids on a regular basis never occurred to me. I found it selfish, logistically impossible, and not worth the effort. I owe the revelation about time away together alone to a dear friend's wedding.

We'd had a couple of weekends where Amanda spent the night at Grandma's before Christopher was born. They were nice and peaceful, but we never went anywhere. It was a luxury just to read the Sunday paper in peace and linger over coffee. Then, three short months after Christopher was born, a dear friend was getting married in New Jersey. I wanted very much to be there. We contemplated dozens of scenarios. I wanted to show off my beautiful children. Try as I might, though, I couldn't escape the fact what would be best for everyone is for Jeff and I to fly out for the weekend without the children.

Leave a three-month-old? Was I out of my breastfeeding mind? The trip required Herculean planning, imposing on Jeff's parents, and pumping a weekend's worth of breastmilk into our freezer (that alone took over six weeks!). I don't think I would have ventured it for any other event than this important wedding.

To this day, however, I am grateful to that couple for teaching Jeff and I the value of time alone away. Lounging lazily by the hotel pool brushing my fingers against Jeff's wet arms as he hung against the poolside, we rediscovered what it was like to be with only each other. We hadn't even realized how lost it had become in the chaos of a new baby. We meandered though shops no stroller would navigate. Nobody drooled on my shoulder (except maybe my husband) for three whole days. We took our time. We chatted in trendy coffeeshops. We ate leisurely, conversation-filled meals. We read. We enjoyed the forgotten (or at least misplaced) pleasure of each other's company in a new and interesting place. I rekindled the romance with my *husband,* not just the father of my children. It was a delicious, magical weekend.

In the hotel elevator, another wedding guest remarked "You look like the cat that ate the canary. What gives?" I asked him if he had any children.

"No."

"Then I'm not sure I can explain it to you." He gave me a baffled look and got off at his floor. I smiled, realizing I had discovered a great secret.

Unless there are pressing reasons not to, Jeff and I try to carve out at least two weekends a year away. Some years it's nearly impossible. Truth is, it's *always* nearly impossible. When I get hung up on the details, I remember that if I pulled it off with a newborn, I can pull it off now. Yes, it means imposing on relatives, swapping with other parents, or even paying someone, but I consider it all time and money well spent. As a very wise woman once said, "Your children can wait while you tend to your marriage. Your marriage will not wait while you tend to your children."

Think about it: What's the first thing you want to know about every job besides the salary? One: What are the hours (i.e. when do I get to go home?)

And Two: How much vacation?

Think about it . . . and plan for yours.

Personal Reflections

1. WHERE in your day does the strain set in? Can you think of some ways to put rest in your day before that straining time? What steps can you take immediately to give yourself a break? What steps will take more planning?

2. THINK about your last vacation. Was it satisfying? Why or why not? What parts of your daily life do you most need a break from? What kind of vacation would make that possible?

3. How can you take a "mental health day" like "slug day"? Are there internal obstacles such as guilt preventing you? External obstacles such as being over-

committed? Think about the last time you were burned out. What consequences do you most regret?

4. THINK about the reasons keeping you from getting away with your spouse. Are they really legitimate or just challenging? What do you think you would gain from an extended time alone with your spouse? What would be the lasting effects of reconnecting for the two of you? For your children?

chapter 5

CHO Employee Benefit #3:
Career Clothes

YOU JUST READ the above chapter title.

Stop laughing, I'm serious.

Nobody talks about this. There is an armload of pregnancy-fashion magazines that give us hoards of details on how to look good while we're expecting. Everyone has spent the last nine months telling us how glowing we look, etc. And here, on our shoulder, is a newborn with a drawer-full of the cutest clothes imaginable. If you are a new mother, this is the time you begin to learn that you are no longer the center of attention. Now that might be putting it a bit harshly, but in fact, once my baby was born, I felt like no one paid any attention to me at all. Sure people told me they came to see me, but let's face it: They were here to ogle the baby. The wise ones knew enough to pay a lot of attention to big sister, Amanda, too, so she didn't feel left out in all the fuss. But for the most part all the spotlights were on my children.

What's this got to do with a mother's career clothes, you ask? It is just one example of the many subtle messages we get that allow us to let our appearances slide. We are exhausted, our milk is just coming in, we're wearing pads we never even knew *existed* two weeks ago, our stitches are still itching, our bellies haven't shrunk *nearly* as much as we'd hoped, and carving out time for a shower feels like it will take an act of Congress.

And let's not even talk about the stains. Amoxicillin and formula manufacturers, are you listening?

It's true, the first few weeks with a baby in the house are killers to a woman's appearance. I can't even tell you how many times I welcomed my husband home from work with the upholstery pattern still imbedded on my cheek from falling asleep on the couch. You know, that bumpy pattern you usually find on your legs from lawn furniture? It's a mighty attractive thing on the face, let me tell you. During those times, you just have to laugh. It is healthy to recognize this as the short season of chaos that it is, and lower your expectations for a while (and perhaps those of your husband).

> How we look sends a message. While it's certainly not the primary source of our self-image, it is a supporting element that can be used either to our advantage or our disadvantage.

You can only do that so long, however, before you start paying the price. It's a price that's very subtle, easy to deny, and deceptively cumulative. We all like to think that as intelligent women, and Christians taught to look on the inside of a person, that we're not all that effected by how we look. But we *are*, because how we look—especially to ourselves in the mirror—sends a message. My experience has been that while it's certainly not the primary source of our self-image, it is a supporting element that can be used either to our advantage or our disadvantage.

I wanted to make sure there was a chapter in this book about clothes because I wish someone had told me about it. Had I been able to look it in the face from the very beginning, I might have taken more care with this issue, and it might have helped my transition.

Winning the War of the Wardrobe

I came from an executive job. Not one where suits were required every day—I suppose it was casual by corporate standards, but I was a manager and executive in my dress and appearance. Most of us who come from that situation do not have a large stock of casual clothes. Things tend to fall to one extreme or another—suits or sweats. Others of you may have had work clothes that clearly defined who you were—nursing uniforms, restaurant servers, etc. Whatever the case, you might find yourself in my position, where three-quarters of what I owned was unsuitable for my new career as a mother at home.

One day I looked around me at Amanda's swimming class and realized that I either appeared overdressed or grungy. The makeup I wore to the office looked overstated for my new surroundings. It dawned on me that a shift to motherhood required just as much image management as a promotion. Again, it's not that I think how I looked changed my value as a mother—I know some outstanding mothers who live in sweats and no makeup. But *I* needed to *like* what *I* saw in the mirror, not feel like a transplanted tree that hadn't taken root yet. To not feel like I was living an unending stream of sick days.

It's that subtle but important difference of making a conscious choice rather than just sloshing along. I needed to create a new look for my new career at home.

I did not, nor would our new smaller income allow me to, rush out and buy a new wardrobe. I could, however, rethink my closet. I began by pulling everything out of my closet and spreading it on my bed. Going piece by piece, I divided all my clothes into "corporate" or "casual." Everything that required dry cleaning—and for some of us, that's a huge chunk of our working wardrobe—went into "corporate," no matter how casual (like some of those really great sweaters). "Corporate" was hauled downstairs to the storage closet. Looking back, this sorting had a healthy ritual atmosphere to it. Once again, I said goodbye to a different season in my life and put it away. Not discarding, but putting aside while I tended to the current season of my life.

I was left with a somewhat empty but more workable closet. Looking at what was left, I could make wise choices about what to do next. I could see that many of my tops from work were still useful, but that it was pants that I needed to buy. And that a couple of bright cardigan sweaters would extend the life of my short sleeve tops—and could be switched without a complete outfit change if someone spit up on them. I could think about how I, as a nursing mother, needed certain kinds of tops that camouflaged milk spots and buttoned to allow for discreet nursing.

> *One morning you open that top dresser drawer and realize you are staring at the lingerie equivalent to flannel work shirts.*

And then there's underwear. One morning you open that top dresser drawer and realize you are staring at the lingerie equivalent to flannel work shirts. Victoria has no secrets here. Somehow you've left lingerie behind and wandered into the drab world of *foundation garments*. If you're really honest, you admit this is looking like stuff your mother used to wear.

Your body has changed considerably. It's time to adjust your unmentionables too. No giggling here, ladies, let Dad watch the kids, leave your modesty behind, and head for the intimate section of a good department store. You have to go to a good, full service department store to find knowledgeable sales people, but this is one case where it's worth the extra money (watch for sales!). Yes, I know for some of us buying bras and underwear ranks right up there with dental check-ups, but remember that most experts will tell you the right bra can not only make you look thinner, it can make you look younger. Again, here's an ally you can't afford not to have on your side.

When the salesperson starts bringing you things that look like they belong on your grandmother, tell her you need a little "umph" in your undies. I had an acting teacher in college who told us to wear red racy underwear to talent auditions. Somehow wearing outrageous garments no one could see gives you mystique. Knowing there's some shiny satin under that sweatshirt could give you just the edge you've been looking for. Great colors, luxurious fabrics, and a good fit are our best enemies against the "frump factor." And as for husbands . . . well I don't think I even need to get into that.

Separating my clothes and augmenting my pared-down wardrobe gave me flexibility and comfort. I could borrow from downstairs for church, special functions, lunch with friends, etc., but my everyday wear was what was in front of me every morning. It was nice not to have high heels staring me in the face as I was getting ready for kindergarten. I worked to find ways to look pulled-together every day because that made me feel good about what I was doing.

The shift came in little things, like needing more colored socks because I was used to gym socks or nylons; belts; and vests that dressed jeans-and-a-shirt up a notch. I, the dragon-lady, found the courage to shorten my nails (but did *not* give up wild shades of polish!). I made adjustments in my make up like changing my black eyeliner to dark gray and taking my eye shadow and lipstick down a few shades to look more natural.

For me, wearing no makeup at all simply made me feel bad. No one else might have noticed, but I would. So I needed makeup that didn't make me look "made up." It's important to recognize this and not to undervalue it. Besides, a visit from the local Avon or Mary Kay lady is just plain fun—and can be done while the children nap! Wanting to look good for yourself and others is not a bad thing.

Hot Buttons and Flags of Defiance

We all have what my mother used to call "hot buttons." Those things that seem to trigger our emotions for good or ill. It's not vanity; it's human psychology. For me, it's my nails. You're laughing again, aren't you? For some reason I cannot explain, if my nails are polished, I feel in control. It doesn't matter if my world is topsy-turvy in reality. Conversely, if my nails look awful, no matter how smoothly life is going, I feel out of control. It's superficial. It's illogical, but most hot buttons are that way.

Why berate yourself over this silly emotional response? I say, use it as your ally. If keeping your nails—or your hair, or your shoes, or your car—in good order gives you a sense of security, than you'd be a fool not to utilize it. We need every bastion of support we can conjure up. Why turn one down just because it's odd?

Take lipstick, for example. A few years ago *First* magazine documented something I had long suspected and our mothers seemed to know instinctively: Lipstick can be a powerful ally. The magazine declared that your mouth *cannot* look tired. It is physically incapable of showing fatigue. Your eyes can betray you in a heartbeat, your body language can scream sleep deprivation, but your mouth cannot look tired.

I found this fact fascinating. Anything on a young mom that can't reveal the fatigue is a treasured asset. It seems my mother was onto something when she told me she'd never leave the house without lipstick. If my mouth can't look tired but my eyes look like a war victim's, I want you looking at my mouth. Suddenly that bright lipstick wasn't out of place; it was my last defense against a face that broadcast to the world I was changing wet sheets at 3 A.M. Somehow, the act of applying a bright red lipstick after a night of horrors is heartening. A flag of defiance. A signal to the world that I may be down, but I'm far from out. Bright red or pink fast-dry-single-coat nail polish is pretty good at boosting your spirits too. Don't forget your toes!

The more I looked for ways to fine-tune my appearance, the more I found. I discovered ways to borrow from my husband's closet to augment what I had. I changed my hairstyle to one that I could pull back in barrettes or a ponytail to occasionally hide "bed hair," because there are some mornings when it is all I can do to get Amanda off to school, much less get anyone else presentably dressed. If you are one of those lucky women who looks good in a baseball cap, you're halfway home—treat yourself to a really cute one and count yourself lucky.

> *Suddenly that bright lipstick wasn't out of place; it was my last defense against a face that broadcast to the world I was changing wet sheets at 3 A.M.*

Perhaps the biggest wardrobe lesson for me, and one that I am sometimes reluctant to talk about, is that I learned that I didn't need to spend what I used to spend on clothes. I discovered the magic of simplicity and a good value. Every time I speak on motherhood, I tell the story of not only me, but my many friends who, after coming home, call me sheepishly to admit, "You know, they have *really cute things* at Kmart!"

Why? Because we'd all never looked before. We were too busy eyeing "better sportswear" in the department store and running our credit cards into the stratosphere. Fashion snobbery—come on, ladies, let's call it what it is—is rather hard to admit. Yet every time I talk about it, I watch dozens of mothers in the audience pop their eyes open as if to say *Oh my, I can't believe she said that! She went through it too! I'm not the only one!* Really, it's okay. There's probably a spectacular second hand store near you just waiting to be discovered. Cut yourself a break and admire your new bargain-hunting skills.

I found it amusing that all this is second nature to women who have always been at home. This was yet another culture shock for me.

The Puffy Truth About Pantyhose

Now I'm feeling brave so I'm going to take the gloves off here. There is another aspect to the clothing issue no one will talk about, and no one will discuss in any pregnancy book. While I know there are exceptions to the rule, it is more likely than not that a large slice of your wardrobe will no longer fit.

Not temporarily, but forever.

While everyone says this isn't true, I meet very few mothers who really get their figures back. The truth is it's a fact of life and age. Don't panic, you can come quite close, but you'll never really have the abs you had—if you had abs at all—before you became a parent. This is especially true with the second or third child. Here is where I think moms at home are at a disadvantage, because you can cover a multitude of sins with control top panty hose. A good strong pair of nylons can get you into almost any pre-baby suit. They've even got those ones with the industrial-strength elastic all the way down the thigh so you can look sleek and smooth under that knit skirt.

But really, do you know any at home moms in nylons? Would you even want to be one?

Spandex exercise leggings are about as close as you can get, and you need to think carefully about where you wear those.

One day you wake up—for me it was unmercifully the same month as my thirty-sixth birthday—and your body has decided it's time for middle age. Poof! Everything shifts from where you want it to where you don't. Every woman I've talked to has had the same experience. Of course, you'll never see this discussed in any fashion magazine, because everybody likes to pretend that you can either prevent it, reverse it, or that is doesn't really happen at all.

And yet it happens. To each and every one of us.

Except maybe to that terribly chic size two in front of me at the grocery store buying organic papaya nectar when I'm buying lice shampoo.

As I see it, you've got one of two choices. You can drive yourself crazy looking at the glamorous lady who's so lean even her hands look slim, or you can pat your puffy belly and remember that the universe's most beautiful children once lived there. You can deny your well-earned flaws (and risk some lumpy leggings) or you can dress to compensate for them.

I'm not saying you should throw in the towel and never see the topside of a Nordic Track again. A healthy mom is the best caretaker of her children. Moderation, however, is the key. In my case, the only way I'll see some of my pre-parent clothes is with a personal trainer, about 20 hours of exercise a week, and a diet fit for a monk. That's not where I want to be spending my time, money, and energy these days.

Sure, I want to look like I used to. Don't we all? I struggle constantly with the balance between what's needed for my health and what my magazine-trained psyche is trying to make me *think* I need. My body can't be forced into something it can no longer be. I had a great figure before I had children, and now I just have an okay figure. Well, maybe okay plus about ten pounds. I could make myself nuts about the ten pounds, or I can be healthy and learn to like my middle-aged self. I can wear things that make me feel good about my body, or I can try to squeeze back into things that belong on a body I no longer own. It was a big step for me to take all my suits to the tailor and have the waists let out an inch or two. It was tough to take my wedding bands to the jeweler and have them sized up. After I did it, though, when I realized how much more comfortable I was, how it wasn't really the life-altering confession I thought it would be, I wondered why I had waited so long.

I can either ask God to help me age gracefully, or I can stock up on control-top panty hose.

I choose—but not without occasional backsliding—the path of grace.

Personal Reflections

1. How did you handle all the attention given to your baby? Were you comfortable, or bothered? Think about how becoming a parent has changed your appearance. Was it for better or worse? Do you feel like you've paid attention to your appearance since becoming an at-home mom? How do you think your husband might answer that question (hint: don't ask him unless you *really* want to know)?

2. TAKE a good look at your closet. Does it reflect your life now? Is your closet a source of stress for you? How does what's inside send a message to you as you get dressed each morning? Do you feel like your clothes match your new career?

3. THINK about how your appearance effects your attitude. Does it have a strong impact? Not much of an impact? How might looking good help you to feel good? Be as honest as you can with yourself about what you've let slide and how you can fix it.

chapter 6

CHO Employee Benefit #4: Raises, Praises, and Promotions

MANY WOMEN MOURN the loss of a paycheck when they decide to move their careers home. I mourned the loss of recognition. The loss of visibility, of perceived importance. I was highly visible in my career and my job and I liked it that way. Like most extroverts, praise motivates me. When I do a good job, I want someone to stand up, take notice, and tell me.

This is, of course, not something you can rationally expect from a five-year-old. In fact, any mother will tell you her children are more likely to complain about the one purple juice cup that is dirty than to notice the 37,000 other dishes that have just been cleaned. My daughter happily steps up to the female tradition of looking at a closet full of just-laundered clothes and declaring she has "nothing to wear"—only because her favorite pair of shorts (worn for two days straight up until this morning) is now in the hamper. Most children will not take the time to thank you for shivering your tail off at the side of the soccer field all fall, but miss one game, and you'll hear about it in spades. The family only notices the one week you just couldn't carve out the time to scrub the bathtub, not the other fifty-one . . . uh, thirty-six weeks you keep it spotless.

And when's the last time one of your offspring ran up and thanked you for those fun-filled eighteen hours of labor? I love the tradition of sending your mother flowers on your birthday—I've done it several times—as a thank you for all the work it took to get you into the world. No one's done it for me yet.

I'm not holding my breath. Let's face it, motherhood ranks as one of the universe's most thankless jobs.

Every once in a blue moon, children express sincere gratitude (not to be confused with the rote response to "What do you *say* to Mrs. Riley for the nice brownie?"). Genuine, voluntary appreciation makes for golden moments, to be sure. But they are so rare. More often than not, when they even try to tell us what kind of job they think we're doing, it doesn't always come out in shining affirmation. Children can be ruthless critics inside smiling faces.

> Children can be ruthless critics inside smiling faces.

Our oven is finicky, which makes broiling and roasting okay, but a finite science like baking often produces mixed results. Our inconsistent oven made it difficult to bake small things like cookies or those biscuits and breadsticks that come in refrigerated tubes. And I'll admit that some nights the chef (i.e., me) is more on top of some things than others. You would think with all the meals that I cook for my family that an occasional slip wouldn't be a problem.

Wrong.

One night I was put in my place by the cheerful but cutting remark of my daughter. I was distracted, and I had left the breadsticks in the oven a bit too long. The tops were fine, but the bottoms had a long strip of dark brown—okay, black—where they touched the cookie sheet. The rest was just fine. I was too tired and everyone was too hungry to care, so I tossed them into a basket (presentation is everything, you know), and set them on the table. "I'm sorry," I sighed as we all sat down,

"Things got away from me and the breadsticks are burned on the bottom." *I'm usually a good cook,* I thought to myself. *They'll understand things can't be perfect all the time. One batch of slightly burnt breadsticks won't do much harm. They get so many good meals.*

My daughter reached out to pat my hand as I pulled my chair in. "That's okay, Mom," she said in a tone I'm sure she thought would make me feel better. "We get them like this *all* the time."

Hmm.

No, the only time you may receive praise for your work is when you march your family into your sparkling bathroom and force them to repeat after you, "Gee Mom, what a clean bathroom! You even got that gross part behind the toilet. Thanks for all that hard work!"

I have actually done this.

As far as I'm concerned, even spoon-fed praise is better than no praise at all. I don't care for my efforts at keeping house to be solely between me and my God.

But that's really part of it, isn't it? The act of staying home to raise your children is selfless in its very essence. We lay aside our worldly gain to invest in things unseen. To be a servant (in the best sense of the word, not the domestic help sense of the word) to a historically unappreciative audience. To a family of burnt breadstick collectors.

Who's Really In Charge Here?

The trick comes in knowing where to look for your motivation. While it's easy to conclude your new boss is that screaming seven month old demanding his seventeenth diaper change of the day, it's the wrong conclusion. He's only the customer. You are serving him, but who commissioned you into this service? Who plans your career path, aids your way, secures resources for you, just like a good boss would?

You probably see where I'm heading with this. If you see your life and your house as driven by your family, you may get points for Customer Service, but you run a high chance of burning out in the process. Your children are not your driving force. Your real boss—the one you need to focus on pleasing and the one with whom you should be having regular communication—is no less than the Creator of the Universe.

I love reminding myself that God in his infinite, perfect wisdom, as a parent himself, selected my children to be raised by my husband and me. We may have chosen to have children, but God chooses the souls that will come into our keeping. Parenthood becomes a journey tailored for our own personal growth, not just the nurturing of our children. If you are looking for importance and influence, try remembering that he chose these precious beings—whom he loved enough to sacrifice his only child—to be raised under your care.

> Parenthood becomes a journey tailored for our own personal growth, not just the nurturing of our children.

That's one plum assignment. God himself has ordained you to this work and you are working on no less than the formation of Planet Earth's next generation. Not to mention heaven's future occupants. This is a high calling, the unseen equivalent of the corner office. You're a Chief Home Officer.

Invoke *that* next time you're picking lint out of the dryer filter.

This makes for nice philosophy, but keeping it up in the daily grind is hard stuff. At first, I couldn't help thinking of motherhood as ordinary—in the bad sense of the word. As in "not special." Over and over I would hear God's tender voice questioning me, *"I loved you enough to send my son to his death for you. You are extraordinary, precious in my eyes. Do you love me enough to be ordinary in the world's eyes?"*

Ordinary? Yes, be an exceptional Chief Home Officer and you will be ordinary. Now, I didn't really like the sound of that. The career gal inside kept complaining that ordinary wasn't a word that applied to young lions like me. I belonged to the movers and the shakers, not the dusters and the scrubbers.

Again the question would echo. *"Do you love me enough to be ordinary if that is what I ask of you?"*

"I don't know, Lord," I'd counter. "I don't like ordinary very much."

"I know."

"I need praise to keep me motivated."

"I know."

"I'm not wired to work unseen, Lord." My hands were on my hips at that point, I'm sure.

"I am the One who wired you. And you are not unseen."

"Okay, I know. But are *you* going to compliment me on my well-dusted furniture?"

The other day my scripture reading included the story of Naaman from 2 Kings chapter 5. Here was another "mover and shaker," a commander in the Aram army. On the advice of a young captive Israeli girl, the Aramian king sent Naaman to Israel to cure his leprosy. Naaman came before Elisha with all his horses, chariots, silver, and gold; and asked to be cleansed. When Elisha sent word—not even personally, but through a messenger—for Naaman to go wash himself seven times in the Jordan, Naaman was angry. Evidently he was expecting something more silver-screen epic. Something a little more spectacular and dramatic. Something not quite so *ordinary.*

Sound familiar?

Well, one of Naaman's wiser servants said "My father, if the prophet had told you to do some great thing, would you not have done it? How much more, then, when he tells you 'Wash and be cleansed'!" (2 Kings 5:13). Sometimes we crave Charleton Heston and the Ten Commandments Hollywood style, but God has asked us to simply go wash in the Jordan. When Naaman followed God's ordinary commands, he was cleansed and became a great believer in God. How much more then should we, when God tells us to, immerse ourselves in the ordinary tasks of keeping a home? It's all about how we define the word "ordinary." I'd like to redefine it to mean "investing in things unseen."

Being "unskilled" for ordinary work is no argument either. I can look at Exodus and laugh at Moses trying to talk God out of sending him to Pharaoh, but did I pay attention when God was calling me to keeping a home when I felt unqualified? The idiocy of my defensiveness struck me months later. God, who formed each cell in my body, who numbers the hairs on my head and knows every sparrow, can certainly notice my clean house. Jesus himself washed feet—a lowly task in biblical times—during his last precious hours on earth. And character is, after all, "what you do when no one is looking." It's not about who's looking. We are in this to serve. It's an integral part of the mystery and misery of motherhood.

I'm not talking about sorting socks for Jesus, but recognizing that this is a large-scale attitude shift for those of us who cut our self-esteem teeth in the working world. Many of us are still Naamans looking for spectacles—and there's a lesson to be learned from that.

Praise Power

While we're on the way to building heavenly character, it can't hurt to have an occasional boost of spirits along the way. Motherhood is a tough job that can all too-easily be written off as unimportant. We would be better off if we recognized our need for earthly praise, and found healthy ways to feed it. Encouragement is a spiritual gift for a very good reason—we need it! In economy-sized doses.

I'd love to think I'll never need praise again, but God has a long way to go with me in that department. I must tread the delicate line between character-building and morale-busting. While I have learned to look to God for my ultimate validation as wife, mother, and ... ugh ... housekeeper, I still actively look for ways to keep me feeling appreciated and motivated.

Enter, the husband. Ladies, take this book directly to your husband and show him the following statement. Remind him that this book is classified as "nonfiction." Ask him if he would mind very much if you tattooed it on his forehead. Hear ye, hear he:

THE MOST EFFECTIVE PRAISE A MOTHER
CAN RECEIVE IS FROM HER HUSBAND.

Until you're not a member of the workforce, you don't recognize the subtle message of the paycheck: "Your work has value. Thank you." Getting that message every week—even if we may not agree with the numerical "value" on that paycheck—helps boost us along.

No paycheck, no boost. Where do we turn?

Praise serves that function for at-home mothers. It says "I know your work has value, and I thank you for your efforts." Nothing—not even chocolate—makes my day more than getting a compliment on my housekeeping or parenting from my husband.

And yes, I've been known to fish for them. I am not above recounting to my husband the list of tasks I have accomplished that day. It helps. Even the simple act of keeping a written list and scratching things off it each day helps. Anything that feeds a sense of accomplishment and celebrates the tiny goals. No, Jeff doesn't *need* to know that I washed the furnace filters or changed the linens, but *I* need someone to know. I want one person over ten years of age on this planet to know that I didn't watch TV or play Barbies all day.

Running a house, if done right, is an almost invisible job. The leaders in the field of Chief Home Officerdom make it look easy. It's done correctly when no one really notices.

Ah, but most of us can't build a life on "no one really noticing." This motherhood business is brimming with situations that can tear you down if you're not careful about keeping yourself built up. Praise is the high-octane fuel of good mothers.

When praise fills your household, everyone wins. Have you considered that your home is the first place your children learn encouragement, teamwork, and compassion? Not only is it good for us to be encouraged by our families, but it's important for them to learn how. At kindergarten open house last night, Christopher's teacher spoke to me not of his mental prowess, his budding penmanship, or how well he lines up every day; she spoke of how CJ offers encouragement and compassion. Math is important, but compassion is priceless. Encouragement beats a well-diagrammed sentence every time. To praise, affirm, and encourage each other is one of the finest skills we can teach our children.

> Praise is the high-octane fuel of good mothers.

Do you remember the last time you were burnt out, frustrated, and feeling under-appreciated? How useful were you? If you're like me, you were not only useless to everyone, you were rather unsafe. We need encouragement and affirmation. We need to know our toil *matters*.

What Matters Most

What is it about the toil that matters? Having just sung the praises of a to-do list, I feel I need to warn you it is a powerfully double-edged sword. If you, like me, try and measure your days by it, you get into dangerous territory. It's a lethal measuring stick for mothers. Some days I get next to nothing accomplished. Nothing at all like the hefty batch of tasks I would churn out in a day at the office. I was used to being "the woman who gets things done!" Yet now there are days where not one thing gets done.

On those days where my house rivals a teenager's bedroom and my lifestyle would send Martha Stewart into convulsions, I try to remember that I did not make this tremendous change in my life to "keep a house." I chose this to "make a home." And making a home sometimes means spending the entire day comforting a sick child or holding a colicky baby. I just this very minute had to force myself to step away from the keyboard so I could help my daughter cut out some doll clothes.

Let us not forget that it also means leaving the dishes sit so you can catch fireflies, trashing the kitchen in a spontaneous confetti snowstorm, or ditching the vacuum to drink chocolate milk inside blanket forts. We're so good at letting our "to-do" lists choke out those moments because we're still thinking with workplace brains. Motherhood is much more about "being" than about "doing." That's hard to remember when no one really sees the "being" part, but the evidence of "doing" is smack in front of your face. Or, unfortunately, it's the consequences of "not doing."

> Motherhood is much more about "being" than about "doing." That's hard to remember when no one really sees the "being" part, but the evidence of "doing" is smack in front of your face.

My favorite mom friend once said to me, "Allie, I like you because you're one of those people who doesn't really care what your house looks like." A backhanded compliment to be sure, but what she meant was that my house was one of fun, not a monument to Better Homes and Gardens.

Chief Home Officers have more on their agendas than keeping house. I am not married to my decorating scheme. I'm not even dating one. My living room still has the paint from when we moved there in 1992. There's crayon on my parquet floors. I let my kids eat off the good china some

Sundays. Our couch is far from spotless because there are days when eating Cheetos on the couch in your pajamas watching cartoons is the *most fun* you can ever have. God called me to employ all my gifts, skills, and energy to raise my children and nurture my family, not to be a "housewife."

The Great Praise Hunt

If your accomplishments can't bring you praise, and your spouse is praise-impaired (not to mention that you shouldn't expect him to be your only source of praise), where do you find it? Well, you find it in very strange and new places. If you tune your mind and your ears, you will find praises everywhere in your household.

Have no doubt: God speaks to you through your children. If you haven't already, you'll have this marvelous experience of hearing God's voice wrapped in the cadence of your little one's words. You must listen very carefully, but I assure you, it will be there.

One night I was tucking Christopher into bed, rocking him, and wallowing in that tender moment when they are drowsy and adoring. It's amazing, isn't it, how they can be devils during the day but turn into the most adorable, love-inspiring creatures as they fall asleep? Christopher and I were laughing softly and recounting the events of his day as his eyelids began to droop. Bending over to slide him under the blankets, I kissed his so soft, so pink forehead. I ran my hand across his curls and whispered, "Jesus loves you, Christopher, and I do too. Sweet dreams." Christopher's gentle hand reached up to grab my thumb as it swept across his brow. He smiled, opening his eyes to look straight into mine, and said, "Jesus loves you too, Mom."

Christopher had never said anything like that to me before. He was only two. I stood still, lost in the moment of love and wonder. And I knew, down to the bottom of my soul, that Jesus *did* love me. As I stood awash in my love for this child, a new, stronger realization came. My God loved me even more than I loved this child. What I feel for these children is but a glimpse of what my Savior feels for me. That's praise. That's affirmation.

Praise is also not just for the getting. It's for the giving. A close second behind the praise of spouses is the praise of fellow mothers. Here is where Hearts at Home is at its most powerful. We are craving affirmation in this isolated profession. Nothing is as uplifting as improving your skills in the company of hundreds of women in the same field. The message of *seeking excellence because our tasks matter* is one we simply can't hear often enough. As mothers, we are in a unique position to know and hold up each other's good qualities. Did you ever stop to think how much better we'd all feel if we spent more time and energy complimenting each other?

> As mothers, we are in a unique position to know and hold up each other's good qualities.

Recently at swimming lessons, a little girl was throwing a terrific tantrum. This little lady was a pro—she had all the tantrum postures and phrases down pat. Like most tantrums, it seemed to be about something so minor that it almost made you laugh. As the spectacle increased, you could just feel the tension mounting. Uncomfortable mothers averting their eyes. The girl's mom just trying to hold it together, to keep a lid on her own growing frustration. You could tell this had been the tenth tantrum this week, if not just this morning. We all just sort of sat there, trying to ignore the child because that's what your *supposed* to do with tantrums right?

Well, yes and no.

The child needs to be ignored. The mother knows all too well we're all thinking about her and trying not to look at her or instead offering her a mildly understanding-but-strained-all-the-same smile. Just because it's the correct way to handle a situation doesn't mean it isn't gut-wrenching. It is so hard to keep your cool when you've got that tornado screaming at your feet.

Finally, I just couldn't take it anymore. I ached for her dissolving composure. I walked over the mother, put my hand on her shoulder, and said, "You're doing an incredible job. I'm not sure I could hold out that long. She'll be president some day with that kind of will-power." We laughed for a moment, and I tried to let her know that we've all been there. You could see the relief in her face. I felt it in my own body.

Parts of motherhood rival active combat, ladies, and we need reinforcements. Do you see a mom in McDonald's really listening to her children? Tell her. Did your friend keep her cool remarkably well when her toddler gashed his head open at the park? Praise her. Even better, praise her in front of her children.

It may be decades before our offspring "rise up and call [us] blessed" (Prov. 31:28). I, for one, can't wait that long without a pep talk. Ask God to give you an encouraging spirit, and never miss a chance to compliment another mother. We need it.

Personal Reflections

1. How do you feel about no longer being a major breadwinner for your family? Take some time and examine what the emotional consequences of leaving the working world have been for you. Are you still feeling valued? Why or why not?

2. WHEN was the last time you paid a member of your family a compliment deeper than "Good Job!" When was the last time you received one? If it's been a while, today is the day to change that by finding reasons to praise your family.

3. CAN you think of a time when it has felt as if God was speaking to you through your children? What was his message? Consider writing these golden moments down so you can revisit them when your spirits are low.

chapter 7

CHO Employee Benefit #5: Training and Development

OWNING THE CORRECT set of chromosomes is not the same as having the correct skill set. This, for me, was the golden secret of motherhood.

We're so loathe to admit it, but we did not come pre-wired for this job. Okay, some of us did, and that's a real gift, but I was not one of them. That didn't make me a bad mother, just an *unskilled* one.

The natural progression of that revelation, then, is that motherhood requires training and development like any other profession. Each mother needs the opportunity to look at her needs and resources, realize the gaps between the two, and then set out to fill them. Pile on top of this the fact that moms are being tested to their emotional and physical limits, and it's easy to see that at-home motherhood is no time to put your brain on hold. As far as I'm concerned, it's the worst possible time to think you can shift into automatic pilot. To excel or even just survive, it's important to tackle this profession with the energy and creativity you once associated with your job. If not the creativity, then the determination and persistence and attention and effort.

But let's face it, wanting to improve your skills and making it happen are two different things. As moms, we're fighting an uphill battle against a lethal onslaught of demands on our time. Being at home is time consuming beyond your wildest imaginations. Don't you hate it when people without children think you're sitting around noshing on bon-bons and watching soaps? We're swamped.

Before you berate those well-meaning but completely uninformed people (who, unfortunately, often are friends and relatives), think about that dreamy point of view. Do you remember how we all *thought* we'd be spending our days once we left the working world? Do you remember how you sat at your desk/counter/workstation and daydreamed about what it would be like once you left the rat race? All the redecorating projects you'd accomplish? Baking gourmet goodies while the children played quietly in the next room in spotless clothes? Even if we already had children, we dreamed about what it would be like to have all that *time*.

> *Motherhood requires training and development like any other profession.*

Doesn't it just make you laugh now?

That daydream is a far cry from the reality of our lives at home, to be sure, but there's a kernel of opportunity in there. We do, actually, have more time now. The trouble comes in how we fill it. I've discovered I need to be careful not to buy into the onslaught of demands. The old adage of tasks expanding into the size of time you have to accomplish them couldn't be more true than on the home front.

Urgent Isn't Always Important

We can take a cue here from some workplace philosophies. Steven Covey, author of *The Seven Habits of Highly Effective People* and *First Things First*, draws the very important distinction between what's *important* and what's *urgent*. Covey champions the tough-to-swallow-but-oh-so-true idea that very often, what's most important isn't what's most urgent. In fact, the most important things are usually the least urgent, because they are large, long-term goals that don't have built-in deadlines.

Urgency is a venerable foe. As mothers of small children, our time is pulled in a thousand different directions. For the first months I was home, I was convinced I'd never have a free moment again. And it wasn't so far from the truth. There are some seasons of chaos, such as those first few weeks with a newborn or when a crisis hits, when our goal needs to be pure survival.

They must be *seasons,* however, not standard operating procedure. Let us never forget that we *have* been given this time at home and it *has* blessings. I believe God's purpose in our being home includes expanding our own horizons.

Take a moment to think about how you view your time. Are you one who operates from a viewpoint of abundance or scarcity? Scarcity tells us there's only enough time for the urgent. Abundance tells us there's time to fit in the important. If we think there's enough time in our day— somewhere—to nurture ourselves, then there will be. More than likely, the more self-nurturing we do, the more effective we'll be at finding enough time to keep it up. Carve out the time to attend a conference like Hearts at Home, and chances are it'll pay for itself tenfold in new energies and ideas. Stephen Covey likens it to the metaphor of "sharpening the saw." Take the time to sharpen your saw, and you'll cut faster. Then you'll have more time to keep your saw sharp, so you'll cut faster, and so on.

Duets

The golden opportunities may have to be mined out of your schedule with effort, creativity, and determination, but the benefits are worth the effort. As you discover those first few nuggets of newfound skills, you will come to recognize that those opportunities are exactly what Mr. Covey was talking about—not urgent, but vitally important.

Sometimes you must start with an irrational leap of faith. This was true for me. One of the craziest things I did after "retiring" was to buy an Irish Lap Harp. I hemmed and hawed for weeks as to whether or not I was kidding myself about having the time to learn a new instrument. Talk about denial! I had a toddler and a preschooler! Did I think they'd all sit happily by, listening to my angelic music while I indulged my fantasy?

Maybe it was denial, but playing the harp was a life-long wish. I'd had a tough year, and it was a beautiful small harp. It was, after all, my thirty-fifth birthday. I finally gave in as a pure act of indulgence. The harp has become near and dear to me for any number of reasons—some musical, some metaphorical. I learned it in tiny steps, in chunks of ten and fifteen minutes carved out of busy days. It took a long time, but I got there.

The harp has more than just musical satisfaction for me. It has come to represent the joyful journey of reinventing myself in this new mom gig. The new, improved, at-home Mrs. Pleiter plays a harp. And that's a good thing.

I fully understood the power of that harp when this year, at age nine, my daughter asked to take harp lessons. I graduated to a full size floor harp, bequeathing her with my smaller lap harp, which just happens to be the perfect size for her. I felt honored to give her something which meant so much to me in so many ways. To know she was as delighted to receive this as I was to give it to her. To pass along the wonder of a new skill to the next generation.

I could not teach her, for I was haphazardly self-taught and needed formal lessons of my own. What we really needed was a teacher willing to teach both of us. God answered my prayers, and led us to a local man who was delighted to take on a mother-daughter team. My breath nearly stopped when he said, "When Amanda gets good enough, we can work on some duets."

Duets.

In all my thrills that Amanda wanted to take up the instrument I loved, it hadn't occurred to me that we could play *together*. What a potent, magical image that became. I thought of her plucking out a simple tune, trying out her new skill; and my underscoring her with the rippling chords of my larger, deeper-sounding harp. I saw this as a wondrous metaphor for our relationship. Even though Amanda's first melodies would be simple, I could add my accompaniment—and, if I did it right—still ensure that her fragile new melody held center stage.

What a potent metaphor for the very nature of parenting.

It will be a joy to watch her melody grow, to take on it's own sophistication and depth as her skills increase. To look forward to the golden moment when we are neither melody nor accompaniment, but true duet, playing off each other. Someday—probably sooner than I think—she'll be grown enough to reach the bottom strings on a full-size harp. Then, I imagine, we'll both graduate to new instruments and find new ways to play together. All because I made the impulsive decision to buy a small harp five years ago. It makes you think there might be only a fine line between impulse and providence.

Don't let yourself buy into the lie that staying home is all about self-sacrifice. Your indulgence in self-nurturing—like mine—may bloom miracles in your children you never imagined.

Just for You, And I Mean It!

Motherhood is servanthood and it involves sacrifice beyond whatever you imagined, but it is lethal to make it all about self-denial. We've all got one in our extended families—those all-out-full-scale martyr mothers. She might have been an aunt, a grandmother, a family friend, or maybe she was even your own mother. Whomever she was, she was a joy-killer. Do you remember how toxic that woman was? How, whether directly or indirectly, she portrayed her time at home as drudgery? The bitterness that would cut a sharp edge around her words?

I believe a dose of self-fulfillment is the antidote for that bitter poison. This season at home is part of God's plan for your emotional, spiritual, and mental development. It may have to come in tiny daily portions, but it can still give you satisfaction. So before you shelve all your personal goals in the name of motherhood, stop and think. Who's to say this season of your life can't also be about finally having enough time to do something you've always wanted to do? In a profession of constant service, it's crucial to do something "just for you."

"Just for you" requires a bit of thought to really make the magic. A manicure or a hot fudge sundae (yes, oh yes!) may fit the bill for a quick shot in the arm, but the *truly* rejuvenating stuff comes when you dip your toes in something that significantly changes you on the *inside*.

That means expanding your brain. Your spirit. I mean things like taking up a craft. Experimenting with a new form of exercise. Learning to cook or bake. Painting. Writing poetry. Restoring the lost art of correspondence. Learning a language. Anything that sparks your imagination and lets you see new possibilities for yourself. The investment is well worth the time.

Neither can we ignore this season of our lives as a golden opportunity for spiritual growth. Even the deepest spiritual volumes can be read in eight-minute snippets in the bathroom. A rich prayer life lies in waiting for those who will sift through the humdrum of a mother's day to find it.

Our church didn't have a mother's group with babysitting so I asked the associate pastor over for lunch and asked if we could start one. Our fledgling group prayed, groaned, and grew together. No mother of small children can get though the day without prayer. And more often than not they are prayers of desperation for patience, perspective, and strength. They are prayers of encouragement when things spin blindly out of control. For trust when children get sick or finances go sour. For wisdom when life gets really messy. God had things he wanted me to learn that I could *only* learn as a mom at home. He still does. I have come to believe that staying at home is as crucial to my personal and spiritual development as it is to that of my children.

Knowledge Is Power

There's a practical side to Mom's Professional Development too. Motherhood and housekeeping require skills—skills that need to be learned and continually improved.

Housekeeping did not, does not, probably will never come to me naturally. When we were first married, Jeff would often take a drinking glass out of the cabinet, look at it, then wash it before using it. There's no getting around it, Jeff is just plain cleaner and neater than I am. One quick look around our bedroom will tell you whose dresser is whose.

> God had things he wanted me to learn that I could <u>only</u> learn as a mom at home.

When I was working, he naturally did a majority of the cleaning because he was better at it. We can both spend an hour cleaning up a room, and I guarantee you Jeff's hour will somehow get the room much cleaner than my hour. This is embarrassing to me. I'm supposed to be better than he is at this kind of thing, right?

I've attended several Hearts at Home conferences out of town. Each time I go, I hear women all around me commiserating about the kind of shape their house will be in when they return. This kills me, because I know, without a doubt to save my self-esteem, that my house will be cleaner then when I left it. Once, just as I was heading out the door, I actually heard my husband say to our kids, "Okay, now we can really get this house into shape." Big, sticky slice of humble pie.

Now that I am home full time, I have a new job description that includes *all* the housekeeping. I mucked around (and I do mean muck) for a few months until a friend set me onto Don Aslett's *Is there Life After Housework?* It is a no-nonsense, practical guide to how to clean and keep a house. I read it from cover to cover. Over and over. I have since found several others, but this still remains my favorite book on the basics.

Much to my glee, this book took a rather business approach to housekeeping. It had a list of what to do when. That's exactly what I needed! A plan. I love plans. I programmed the book's housekeeping schedule into my electronic organizer. You may be laughing, but I know that if it's not on a list I'm lost. If my to-do list doesn't actually *tell* me to clean the refrigerator, I have learned that I will not look at the refrigerator and think, *Well, this needs cleaning.* My brain just doesn't work that way. I could not rely on my instinct to get the job done.

I had to wise up to the fact that I needed to *learn* this skill.

This isn't such a foreign idea, just a foreign application. Think about it: If I had been asked to use a new computer program at work, I wouldn't dream of sitting down in front of my monitor expecting the procedures to come to me by osmosis. I'd grab a manual, take a class, or find the instruction I needed to get proficient.

This new job description is no different. It's robbing yourself to do any less with the many skills required for motherhood. You've got to *learn* them. But where? Some of us have extended families nearby that have mentored us from the beginning. I, like most women these days, didn't. That mentoring process rarely happens naturally within families anymore. So we, as professionals, need to give nature a jump-start. Here's where women continually hold up the Hearts at Home organization as their only source of "mommy school." Motherhood 101. What could be more relevant for us than a conference devoted entirely to the training and development of at-home mothers?

It's not just conferences that send us home with books and tapes. The world is brimming with hidden teachers on the fine art of motherhood. One day, when we finally had the guts to admit to each other how hard it was to keep house, our church's mothers group hit upon a simple but astounding idea. We asked a group of older women renown for their housekeeping to come and share the tricks of the trade. What an affirmation for the older women; what an education for us rookie moms! Some of the advice I received that day changed my life significantly. In addition, it was wonderful to hear from those older moms that they felt things were harder for us these days. The harsh realities of today's society means our kids are much more underfoot then we were to our parents. It was encouraging to have women say how much they respected the challenges we faced.

Find those who are good at what you need to know and let them share their knowledge. Chances are you will both be blessed and you may end up with a new friend in the process.

I have always been a good cook, so I did not need to learn cooking, but I burned a lot better than I baked—you already know about my success with breadsticks. One trip to the local bakery to order a cake for my daughter's birthday party, however, was all the incentive I needed to change that deficit. Appalled at the prices for even a small bakery cake, I headed straight for the library and checked out a stack of books on baking and cake decorating. But it's smart to know your limitations—I make my own cakes but I use a box mix. I figure the payoff's in the frosting, so that's where I spend my time and energy. I decorated a cardboard box as a practice run for my first birthday party cake before I let myself near the

> *Find those who are good at what you need to know and let them share their knowledge.*

real thing. I'm still no Martha Stewart, but I can do a good enough cake to please a small army of 6-year-olds. And I harbor no small amount of pride that I pulled it off. I take a picture of every cake I decorate.

I, who used to frighten house plants, have planted a bulb garden with the help of a friend famous for her green thumb. All it took was a call to her with an invitation to share a cup of coffee and her know-how. She came over bursting with books, ideas, and enthusiasm. If you're cheerful about it, people will teach you anything. I trotted into the local garden store with a map of my front yard and some clippings of flowers I liked from my friend's bulb catalogs. The guy at the store spent an hour with me, walking me through the process and even drawing me a "plant by numbers" map. I had instructions to plant the bulbs in bag 1 in area A, etc. You can imagine my pride when the crocuses and daffodils came popping their colorful heads out the next spring. I've been back twice a year ever since. It's not a fabulous garden, but it's fun, I'm enjoying it, and I get a little bit better each year.

I had not thought about the fact that my children had watched me engage in this experiment until the next year, when Amanda asked for her own garden. She had been watching me take risks, admit my inexperience, learn, and try. We were a sight that next spring, Amanda and I, trying to figure out how to dig up the grass from the tiny plot she'd chosen. Neither one of us could find a way to get below the grass roots to tear back the sod. I don't think you are supposed to cut the turf out with hedge shears, but that's what we ended up doing. I'm sure it was a comical sight—the botanical blind leading the botanical blind. Amanda chose her own annuals, plotted out their placement, and watered them as faithfully as any six-year-old does anything. She showed her garden to anyone who would look, with great pride. When she didn't show it off, I did. Our gardening gloves hung side by side in the garage.

You'll find, to your amazement, that one small success breeds an appetite for more. One summer I learned how to barbecue for the first time in my life. I held up my tongs with just as much zeal as my pastry bag, proclaiming myself the newly installed "barbecue babe." I've learned how to do our taxes. Taken up knitting. Tried a dozen different forms of exercise. And, perhaps most amazing of all, launched a writing career. Sure, I do my learning in small slices between parenting tasks, but that doesn't dilute the joy. A new skill is an irreplaceable treasure. What better way to truly show our children the joy of learning? To display for them that God's world is full of wonder just ready to be explored.

Sneaky Skills

Some aspects of motherhood are easily identified as skills. Other things we assume are character traits, gifts, or talents rather than learnable skills. For me, entertaining children is a prime example of this. Despite a degree in theater, entertaining children does not come naturally to me. Ideas for fun would never appear in my head in response to the dreaded moan, "I'm bored, Mom!"

It took me almost a year before I figured out that this too is a skill to be learned. This stuff takes planning, salesmanship, and a hefty supply of the right materials. Again, there are some mothers who have a gift for this kind of thing, but the rest of us need to get intentional about it. How do you learn to be fun? Not just any fun, but fun to a five year old? This loomed a big problem to me.

There's a lot more out there on this particular topic than you think. After going through the humbling step of admitting my incompetence (ouch!), I began to scour parenting magazines for craft ideas. I checked out activity books from the library. I discovered a gem of a PBS show called "Donna's Day" which devoted a half hour each week to fun things to do with your family. Who knew you could paint toast with milk and food coloring?

Never able to come up with this stuff on the spur of the moment, I installed a "project box" in a corner of our house and filled it with craft supplies, ideas, egg cartons, etc. I hunted through the now-numerous home-schooling stores for paints, workbooks, clay, etc. I made a list of projects and stuck it in the inside of a cabinet door, vowing I would have at least three answers whenever anyone moaned about having nothing to do.

Moms, be warned: Even this is not enough. Like all good children, Amanda soon knocked the wind out of my sails:

"Mom, I'm bored. I don't have anything to do."

"Okay, let's make bead bracelets."

"No."

"How about egg-carton flowers or caterpillars?"

"That's boring. I want something *really fun* to do."

"We could bake cookies."

Said in a tiresome voice while rolling on the floor: "Moooooommmmmm, that's no fun. I want something fun!"

So I haven't won the battle. But I have a lot better artillery now. And a battle plan that will knock your socks off—if I don't make puppets with them first.

Personal Reflections

1. IN what areas did you come "pre-wired" for this job? What strengths and talents did you bring to motherhood? What are the areas where you feel you need "training"? Is it hard or easy to admit you lack those skills?

2. WHERE in your personal growth do you feel God is calling you to improve? What do you think God might be waiting to teach you in this season at home?

What feelings or circumstances are telling you that there's not enough time for that kind of growth? How can you combat those?

3. TAKE a moment to list all the things you'd love to do "if you had time." Give yourself the freedom to dream a little, to be unrealistic. Are any within reach—even in small steps? See if you can find one or two that you can start this week, even if it's as small as ordering a catalog or buying an instructional book.

chapter 8

CHO Employee Benefit #6:
Colleagues and Coworkers

I HAVE HAD two children bodily attached to each of my legs and never felt more alone.

On the one hand, I loved the unhurried contact, the lazy togetherness of being home with my children. But day after sleep-deprived day can wear on a soul. The sheer vacuum of it all was nearly stifling those first few months away from work. Not silence and stillness—these things are luxuries to me now—but the incessant, invasive flood of noise, activity, and body contact associated with babies and small children. This was a brand of human interaction with the potential to be far more irritating for me than stimulating.

Our children can hand us golden moments of extraordinary truth and love. Having the time to watch your baby fall asleep before your eyes is nothing short of magical. To sit on the back deck and blow bubbles just because the weather seemed perfect at that exact hour is a precious thing. Your little one can stop you dead in the tracks of an ordinary conversation with something awe-inspiring.

Christopher gave me one of those marvelous gift-of-a-moment times when he was two. It was a gray fall day, full of nondescript errands and chores. We were sitting together at a small table near the window of our kitchen, sharing lunch. I don't even remember what we were "discussing." Suddenly, the sun found its way out from behind a cloud for the first time that day. Our kitchen is filled with wood cabinets, so when the sun comes in the whole room changes color, taking on a golden glow.

I hadn't even noticed it until my eyes caught Christopher's face. His expression stopped my forkful of salad halfway to my mouth. His countenance was angelic. Complete and utter joy—in that astounding intensity that seems to be the unique capability of small children. Holy. His face looked holy as he basked in the light, his small face upturned in thanks to the skies, his eyes closed. I nearly gasped.

"Sunshine," he said, savoring the word. It struck me at that moment that I had just witnessed my son's first act of worship. He was, in his basic, toddler way, praising the Creator for that lush slice of sunlight on an otherwise gray day. Yet, what gift of sensitivity had allowed me to see it that way? Why did my mind attach such importance to such an everyday thing? I received my answer when I thumbed through my journal later that afternoon and found a prayer I had written the prior week. I had prayed that I might have the joy of watching my son praise his Maker. Indeed I had. I assure you my outlook on a gray day has changed forever.

Overcome and Out the Door

Surely, moments like those do happen. But they are so rare. In fact, they are often wrapped in mounds upon mounds of minutia, demands, irrationality, questions repeated ad nauseum, endless choruses of "Mooommm!" and just plain hysterics. In endless strings of colds and ear infections. In drawers repeatedly opened and emptied, books pulled from shelves, and last-minute searches for Mr. Teddy because someone simply *cannot* sleep without him even though it's already half an hour past bedtime.

Our tool in finding those golden moments, in catching them before they fly by, is perspective. Without perspective, we'd drown in the daily drudgery, in the sheer ordinariness of it all. We may be CHOs, but we've got the top post at a company completely operated by little employees who won't listen to reason. Some of whom don't even understand a single word we say. We are left coping with elements far beyond our control. There are no rules. No back-up support. Nowhere to find that vital perspective.

We are convinced we are out here in enemy territory alone.

Until we reach out.

Every single one of us has had those days where the reality of full-time motherhood is so much more frustrating than we would have ever dreamed possible. Where the urge to run away is stronger than you thought any *good* mother could have. Where everybody's sitting on the kitchen floor crying, including you. I had one rock-bottom moment where I realized my watch was so soaked with spit-up that it smelled too gross to wear. My *watch*. I mean really, what cubic volume of breastmilk are we talking about when it is sufficient to saturate a *watchband*?

The seemingly permanent eau de breastmilk and rice cereal had invaded every square inch of me. I stared at my watch's now whitewashed-but-once-lovely leather band and felt my heart puddle at my feet. My pretty, adult-looking watch, the last bastion of my former grown-up life (the earrings and nice clothes having been retired weeks earlier), saturated beyond repair with regurgitated breastmilk. I felt like it ought to be pasted in the dictionary right next to the word "pathetic." Amanda was tired and cranky but refusing to take a nap—it's not something four year old's like to put *back into* their lives no matter how much their little brothers wail all night long. Christopher was just kicking into the "arsenic hour." I was so tired I could have slept on the sidewalk.

I felt utterly alone. Defenseless. Overcome. Jeff was working long hours that summer and it would be as much as three hours before he'd walk in the door. Everyone else on my block was still at work. I loved my children, but I was convinced I would never see the light of an un-spat-upon day again. There, leaning up against the refrigerator on my kitchen floor, blowing my nose on paper towels, I didn't know what to do.

But I learned. Desperation is a good teacher.

While prayer is certainly the balm of desperate mothers, I know—now—that when I'm feeling like the only mom in the universe and the baby's wailing for no consolable reason, I need to pick up the phone. Or tuck the screaming little darling into a stroller and head out the door. If I stay at home because I think my kids are too impossible to take anywhere, things will usually only get worse. Somehow, someway, things always improve (even if its only my disposition) on the other end of a phone conversation, a walk, a lap around the mall, or even an ill-advised pre-dinner trip to the ice cream shop.

Late one sweltering summer afternoon Amanda, Christopher, and I sat dipping into an obscenely large chocolate sundae at the dairy store. It was near dinnertime, and I was trying hard to ignore the downward glances of nutrition-conscious mothers who were there for hormone-free milk or some other worthy purchase. *Yes*, I wanted to shout, *I know very well I'm breaking all the rules.*

All of a sudden, a joyful looking old man walked by our table and smiled at me. Not scowled, just smiled. I was grimy, had circles under my eyes, and was trying to keep the majority of the ice cream in or near the bowl. "Looks like you've earned that!" he said with an "I've been a parent too" look on his face. No judgements, no nutritionally-based scorn, just understanding. Perhaps he will never know how he lifted my spirits that day. I *had* earned it. We had survived a really tough afternoon. We all earned the privilege of eating hot fudge before dinner that night. I felt buoyed for someone having recognized my toil. Understanding the tiny victory that needed celebration.

Far better than phone or fudge, however, is the company of other moms. I have slumped into mother's fellowship meetings, puffy-eyed and bed-haired, sneering, "Anybody wanna buy a kid cheap?"

"Which one, Allie?"

"Either," I hiss, falling into a chair. "Buy one, get one free."

Then I laugh. They all join in and I catch the eyes of women who know exactly how I feel. And it gets a little better. Even a frantic lunch date in McDonald's supervising squirming children is a precious lifeline. Knowing there is someone *else* in the world who can't get through half a sandwich without a crisis makes it easier. Watching someone else try to eat with one hand while holding a fussy baby gushes forth a balm of familiarity.

> Then I laugh. They all join in and I catch the eyes of women who know exactly how I feel. And it gets a little better.

Why is it we seem to forget this basic human truth and instead hunker down at home when the going gets rough? Why do we think no one else can stand our kids when we're on the verge of—or past—standing them ourselves? Only another mother understands that we adore them, we'd give our lives for their well-being, but it'd be really nice if they were somewhere else for a few hours. Why do we convince ourselves we can't hold a phone conversation while the baby is crying when as often as not the sound of our voice talking to someone else calms them down? I can't even begin to count the number of times I started a phone conversation with a screaming Christopher and finished it with him asleep in my arms.

Whatever soul out there invented the cordless phone, I want to shake your hand.

God knew what he was doing when he didn't leave Adam alone in the garden. By our very created nature we are beings of community. We are imperfect women who need the help and support of one another. Where we get into trouble is when we think we don't need each other. That if we are mature, healthy adults, we ought to be able to handle it.

I believe part of the problem comes from what I call "The Myth of Not Working." We as at-home moms are living the ideal, right? We still can't convince ourselves to admit this new job is as tough—if not far tougher—than the one we left. After all, what kind of a woman would admit to incompetence as a *mother*? We're supposed to come genetically wired for all this, right? It's in the instinct. Some of us have been longing to do this for years. We made this heroic choice and we wouldn't dream of letting on that we can't quite pull it off yet. We *get* to stay home all day. We are spared from slugging it out in the workforce, right? Who are *we* to complain?

> We still can't convince ourselves to admit this new job is as tough—if not far tougher—than the one we left.

We are the women with the toughest, most important job in the universe, that's who.

Knowing Where to Turn

I called a friend one day absolutely beside myself because Amanda's preschool carpool fell through the day before school started. All I could see before me was a long line of stuffing infant Christopher into snow suits in sub-zero Chicago January to drive Amanda the two and a half minutes to and from preschool twice a day. Not to mention waking the poor fellow smack in the middle of his morning nap. In my world, this was a major crisis. With only one day before the start of school, all the other moms were sure to have had their car pools all worked out so there'd be no one left for me. I was despondent.

Now, no other mother of a post-colicky infant would have belittled this dilemma. But I called a working friend who was not a parent. After a palpable silence on the other end, she gave me the equivalent of "holy cow, girl, try and find something real to worry about" and went on about her daily business. I was stung. I felt petty and insignificant. I sat on my kitchen counter and pronounced my stint as an intelligent citizen over. I was demoted to way, way down on the food chain.

An hour or so later a mom friend called about something else. I bemoaned my fate to her. She understood immediately and completely. Because she was a "colleague," she could see that this turn of events was going to have a serious impact on nearly every day of my life for the next nine months. She knew the particular agony of having to wake a sleeping baby. She commiserated. She encouraged me. She helped me think of some possible ways out of that mess.

A lawyer wouldn't call an accountant to help her sort out a sticky legal problem. As moms of small children, we need other moms. We need moms with kids just our own kids' age. We need moms with children a year or so older. We need moms with children much older. We need each other because this *is* the hardest job in the universe and you cannot leave it at the office.

Amanda was two and a half and just getting the potty thing when we took a driving vacation. Well, it was supposed to be a driving vacation, but it felt more like a stopping vacation. I dubbed that summer "The Potty Tour," because we saw the inside of nearly every public restroom from Chicago to Connecticut. Potty training in the privacy and comfort of your own home is one thing. Hitting the mark in a public restroom— and a highway rest-stop bathroom at that—is another story.

The real villain in this story is the automatic flushing mechanism. That gizmo would invariably go off with Amanda's tiny little bottom still on the seat, making a sound so loud she feared she would be sucked into the plumbing at any moment. After the second episode, I could barely get her in the stall without an argument. By the end of the trip I was sure she'd end up in therapy and Depends.

On the next to last day of the trip, another mother overheard our now daily tirade as I tried to convince Amanda the commode would not eat her alive. She walked over to me and whispered, "There's a sensor on the back wall. It's that red-black circle there. Just cover it with your hand and the toilet won't flush." The pearl of great price. The most important piece of information I learned all year was handed to me over the sink on Interstate 80. I would have hugged her if I weren't so busy beating myself up for not having figured it out two days and 800 miles ago. Whoever you are, my child is a well-adjusted nine-year-old in purple underwear because of your compassion. A thousand thanks.

> We need each other because this _is_ the hardest job in the universe and you cannot leave it at the office.

We're all in this together. The golden truth in all this is that the battle-trench friendships you forge with other moms are some of the strongest of your life. While you are home, you can actually have the time to grow and nurture those friendships to a depth you may never get again. You may get the chance to deepen an existing friendship. You may have to take a deep breath and go out and find yourself some new mom friends. Yes, that feels awkward and it's scary, but it is worth it.

Expand Your Staff

Mother friends are an invaluable asset. It is dangerous and unhealthy to expect your spouse to provide all your support. Studies have related that a woman's network of support should include at least five friends, including one or two really close friends. I like to think of them as my coworkers, the staff I can turn to for support. It takes different kinds of friends to fill different kinds of needs. Near as I can figure, it's best of all when you have one of each of five kinds of friends:

1. THE TWIN: This one's in the exact same boat as you. Your children are close to the same age, and you're at the same point in your life (this doesn't mean you have to be close in age). Chicken pox struck your house within days of each other. Your kids potty trained—or even worse, failed to potty train—the same summer. The one you can call up and say "I just found my first wrinkle. How soon can you get here if you stop off at the ice cream store on the way?"

2. THE SPARKLER: Everyone could use one crazy friend. Sometimes it's helpful if this one isn't a parent (or doesn't have really young ones), because they can remind you that some people in the world can still be spontaneous. This is the one who'll call you up to go see a French film without subtitles just because the hero is drop-dead gorgeous. Who actually bought flare jeans when they came into fashion. Or is the kind of person who'll convince you to go out in public wearing your daughter's blue sparkle nail polish. Hands *and* toes.

3. THE ROCK: She's unflappable. Nothing ruffles her feathers. She can bring you back to earth when you're convinced your world is falling apart. She's the woman to turn to when it all hits the fan because she'll know just what to do. The kind of woman who doesn't just *call* when your basement

has flooded and your kids have the chicken pox. She *shows up* with bleach, oatmeal, eight Blues Clues videos, and a complete cooked meal.

4. THE BEEN-THERE FRIEND: This woman has children older than yours. It can be two years or seven years. The one who can say "Oh yeah, I remember when Jessica's diapers turned that color. Don't sweat it." The one who can tell you what's best to pack in a first grader's lunchbox, where to get those itsy-bitsy bottles of glue you need for kindergarten when every store is out of stock, or which department stores have the best women's rooms to nurse in. I have found this woman to be particularly priceless when your children are eight, nine, or ten and she has teenagers. Talk about perspective!

> This season of our life hands us the best opportunity to take friendships far beyond the surface.

5. THE BEST FRIEND: New friend or old, it makes little difference. You know this person's connection to you in a heartbeat. You can cry in front of her. You can call her and scream when your husband's done something atrocious and you need to vent. The one you can call at 2 A.M. when you need to go to the emergency room. She can see you without your makeup. You can go *bathing suit shopping* with her. You can have fun even at the laundromat as long as you're with her.

My list of friends doesn't look like this. It's an ideal. But I find the idea of a "staff" of different kinds of friends useful. It forces me to think about the people in my life and what might be missing. It keeps me from relying completely on my husband for all my earthly emotional support. It reminds me that it's up to me to build my own personal safety net, and how much richer my life is when it's in place.

The friendship of mothers is the lifeblood of our vitality. We need to *have* friends. We need to *be* friends. You can hand someone the hint that will save their summer. Or discover what it is like to step in as Christ's earthly hands and feet, serving as the answer to another mother's prayer for help. This season of our life hands us the best opportunity to take friendships far beyond the surface. You have the chance to invest in what really, really matters. Don't pass it by.

Personal Reflections

1. TAKE some time to reflect on the "miracle moments" of your parenting. If you can, write them down. Are they as rare as we think, or would we find more if we were more attuned to looking for them?

2. WHAT do you do when you hit rock bottom? Is your first impulse always the best one (I'm thinking about ice cream here. . .)? What are some of the more useful responses you could have? Is there anything stopping you from taking those measures?

3. How is your friendship "staff?" Does it need a little expansion? Who is the woman you can begin a friendship with who might fill in the gaps? Where can you go in your community or church to meet some new friends? Are you taking the time to nurture the friendships you have? Are there friendships you need to let go of?

chapter 9

CHO Employee Benefit #7: Sick Days

ASK ANY MOM what the worst part of staying at home is and you'll probably get the same answer: being sick while you're still trying to take care of children. It's hard to decide which is worse: taking care of sick kids while you're sick too or trying to deal with healthy kids while you're on your deathbed. Both are particular tortures of motherhood.

Sick days were one of the luxuries of day care. Even if I had to pull over twice on the way, I would crawl to day care with Amanda so I could go home to rest in a quiet house. These days are gone. How do you handle it when you are sprawled on the bathroom floor getting sick into the toilet and your two-year-old is poking you in the back saying "Whadda doing, Mama?" How do you explain to a four-year-old that if he elbows you in the stomach one more time you're going to redecorate the couch? Screaming children are no balm for headaches. And illness does nasty things to tempers. Short fuses abound when viruses lurk around the house. Just about every family I know has been at that loathsome point where two spouses are arguing about who's sicker so the other has to watch the kids.

Golden Moments in the Germ Warfare

Believe it or not, it's not all bad. There can be bright sides to children learning about a sick mommy. Children learn to care, to nurture, and even if they are a bit over-enthusiastic about it, this is a good place for them to learn to comfort.

I've had a few golden moments in all the germ warfare. I am a frequent sufferer of migraines, so really bad headaches are an unfortunately big part of my life. Some are easy to overcome with the help of medicines; others are more of a struggle. While it is awful, it has opened windows for me to be reminded that my children do possess extraordinary compassion.

One day I was crumpled on the couch, struggling miserably through a headache which simply would not subside. My husband was kind enough to stay home just a few hours that morning, hoping that the second dose of medication might do the trick, and was rounding up the children to go outside so I could have some peace and quiet. As he herded then two-year old Christopher and six-year-old Amanda outside, Christopher doubled back to fetch something from his room.

I expected a truck or ball to reappear around the corner with my son. Instead, he returned with not one, but both of his blankets from his crib. He trotted over to the couch, a heart-melting smile on his face, and stuffed them into my arms. "Okay now, Mama" he pronounced, and planted a squishy kiss on my aching forehead. Here I was thinking Christopher was too young to understand that I was sick, and he was proving me wrong. He knew Mommy didn't look right. With a lurching heart I realized he'd lent me the best remedy he knew. He was extending comfort to me from his own world. It was one of the priceless, timeless moments God gives us as mothers—often when we are at our wits end and ready to give up. This act of pure compassion healed me more than any of my prescriptions, for it contained a hefty dose of peace. I wrapped myself up and inhaled the unmistakable, exquisite scent—that baby smell we all know in a heartbeat. I fell asleep for an hour or so, giving my body the time and rest it needed to allow the medicine to work. I awoke feeling much better. But most of all, that potent blessing—at the tiny hands of my toddler—gave me the strength to get through the rest of my day.

Of course, this is the Hallmark card of sick days. Rare and wonderful. But rare. Excruciatingly rare. Far more often, our sick days are ugly torture sessions that test us to our very bones. Sometimes you feel as if it's out there, just waiting for you, like a sniper in the bushes. It *is*. As mothers, we live in a festival of germs from preschool to the playground, from the backyard to the pediatrician's waiting room. We get sick. One child gets sick. Then the other. Our husbands get sick. And sometimes, on the cruelest of days, it is all of the above.

> *We get sick. One child gets sick. Then the other. Our husbands get sick. And sometimes, on the cruelest of days, it is all of the above.*

One January—doesn't this kind of thing always seem to happen in January?—every member of my family was terribly sick. For four straight days. Even Jeff's parents—the only family we could have called on to come rescue us (believe me, we thought of it)—were sick. Jeff and I were so sick we couldn't even sleep in the same bed. Every night, just minutes after we'd finally coaxed the last sick child to sleep, I'd slump down the stairs to our fold-out couch in the den, sit on the edge, and cry for the dread of doing it all over again the next morning.

What's a mother to do?

Plan.

Battlestations!

No human resource department hands you a pre-scribed allotment of sick days for moms. You have to go out and make them. Like Scarlett O'Hara against the sunset, I swore I'd never live through a January like that one again. I called a friend and made a "sick day pact." If I was too sick to take care of my kids, I'd call her. If she was too sick to care for her children, I'd take them. We gave each other permission to ask huge favors, to put each other out, and inconvenience our families. We both stared at each other over our coffee mugs and wondered why we didn't think of this before.

Why didn't we? If we would be too sick to go to work, aren't we too sick to be responsible for our children? Again, I believe it's the myth that we aren't really working. After all, how hard can it be to sit on a couch and watch your kids play? I *know* you know the answer to that question.

For those of you who are first-time parents, this is a good place to point out one of the basic, naked truths about parenting: Some of it is just plain awful. It doesn't mean that you're going about it wrong, or you've done something to paint yourself into a corner, or you've not taken steps to avoid a situation, it's just that parts of it are hideous. Sounds obvious, but it's one of those things babies have to teach you.

When Amanda was first born, she would cry every day in the late afternoon. I know now that this is perfectly normal behavior for babies. "The Arsenic Hour" didn't get its name out of thin air. But I, Problem Solving Mother that I was, called my midwife to ask for advice on helping Amanda (and, I admit, me) through this trouble spot in my normally affable child's life. I heard her sigh on the other end of the phone. "Allie," she said, "babies cry in the late afternoon. Babies in China cry then. Babies in Africa cry then. It's just something babies do." She awakened me to the fact that some things you just have to slug through.

When I asked a seasoned parent friend about breast-feeding, her casual reply was, "Once the scabs heal, it's really no big deal."

This ground my consideration of nursing to a screeching halt. *Scabs?! No one said anything about scabs?!? Scabs are things that cover WOUNDS!! Wounds involve lots of pain. I don't like pain.* Nursing hurts the first few weeks for most of us. In a place we *really* don't want to experience pain. After than initial adjustment period, though, it really is "no big deal." Again, we assume it comes to us automatically, when actually there's a huge learning curve for both Mom and baby.

Nursing was one of those "gut through it" things for me. Amanda was a champion nurser (she earned the nickname "Hoover baby" from us), but the first two weeks were painful and difficult. I have encountered scores of other mothers since then whose stories match mine. You simply gritted your teeth (literally!) and stuck it out until it got better. And it did. Granted, sometimes you need to know when to cut your losses and try something else, but for the most part, parenting is a powerful lesson in the value of persistence.

Pain for your children, well that's an entirely different story. The time you must watch your helpless, tiny, wailing child slug through the tough parts is worse than anything you may endure on their behalf. You're helpless to stop it or keep your child from it. Any mom who has learned how to clamp her legs around a screaming child and hold his arms down while he gets his *four* kindergarten shots knows this to be true.

Every parent of a colicky child knows that low moment when you stop trying to even find a bright side to it. That horrible feeling in the pit of your stomach as you drag your body to bed, knowing that all-too-soon a gut-wrenching cry will thrust you onto the night shift. I spent every night of our first week at home holding a sobbing little baby. There is no way around colic, no way under it, or over it. You only plow through it.

Why do I mention all this? Because some days with sick kids—or especially with sick moms—are just plain torture. You're better off not kicking yourself for not taking steps to avoid them because they are unavoidable. They happen and they're awful. Surrender, folks, the germs have us outnumbered.

Technology Is Your Friend

I can't talk about illness without discussing your number one ally in this nasty battle: the VCR. I would like to think I am careful about my children's daily television intake. On the other hand, illness is one place where all bets are off. As I see it, this is exactly why God had us invent the VCR.

One very smart mother I know has a set of several six-hour videocassettes of her children's favorite—and acceptable—TV programs. You know what I mean—a couple of days worth of the local PBS station's morning or afternoon scheduling. She takes advantage of the extended play speed on her machine so that it's all on one tape. I've followed her example. Once or twice a year, I make new tapes—two or three of them. That way, when I'm ill or they're ill, we can pour ourselves on the couch and watch. If you haven't done this, remember that if your children are toddlers or younger, they might actually *enjoy* watching *Elmopalooza* six times in a row so you might not need to make one long tape of different shows. I know a mom who, when she was very ill, learned that her active toddler son could actually watch the same two-hour movie five times in a row and not end up in therapy. For that matter, your children might actually consider it as a treat (although talk about making *you* miserable)!

The November Amanda was four and CJ was still a baby, the chicken pox struck our house with a vengeance.

Amanda came down with a whopping case of it. CJ would surely follow.

The next day the VCR broke.

This, in my view, was a crisis of gargantuan proportions. After an hour or so of pure panic, I hit upon a plan. I called the local high-end electronics store—you know, the kind who let you loan out the equipment so you can try it out in your home before you buy it. Not the discount appliance place, but the stereophile type of store. The most important thing I did was ask to speak to a parent—*any* parent—on staff. I needed someone with sympathy and understanding on the other end of that phone. I explained my dire situation to a salesman and within minutes we had crafted an attack. I gave him all the pertinent information—including my credit card number and my best attempt at describing the machine's problem—on the phone ahead of time. Then I piled the kids into the car (I believe I needed to promise a detour into McDonald's drive-thru to accomplish this), pulled up to the store's entrance, and honked three times. My hero came out, handed me the paperwork through the driver's side window (which included a knowing sigh of battle-trench camaraderie), popped open my hatch, took the damaged machine for repairs, and replaced it with a loaner from the store. I called him from home and he walked me though installing it on the phone.

Now any ordinary, sane adult might have thought this extreme. But a parent knows that a distracted sick child is much easier to deal with than a bored sick child. Sometimes what you need most is battle-worn parents who know where the real crises are. As it turned out, our house was on quarantine with the chicken pox and subsequent viruses for forty-three straight days, including Thanksgiving.

Gather Your Allies

You need more than just a sympathetic VCR salesman on your side. It's a good idea to gather your allies before the virus strikes so you're prepared when things get ugly.

One of the best pieces of advice I received out of a baby book was to find and make friends with the local drugstore. Not the giant-attached-to-the-grocery or discount-store kind, but the neighborhood drugstore. This may be a challenge if you've got insurance issues, because sometimes it's difficult for those little stores to deal with all the insurance paperwork, but it's worth the effort.

Most importantly, find a pharmacy that delivers.

Few tortures are worse in this life than clinging to the pharmacy counter, trying not to throw up waiting for your prescription while your toddler is busy rearranging the toothpaste in the next aisle. The same pharmacy that can deliver your amoxicillin can bring you a small package of diapers, aspirin, tampons, etc. while you're holed up with a host of germs. Knowing the guys at the local store allows you to laugh while you're picking up the fourth prescription for antibiotics in six weeks because yet *another* member of your family has come down with strep. You can make those embarrassing "Can I take this while I'm still taking that?" or "Is her urine *supposed* to turn that color?" calls and know the person on the other end of the line actually remembers who you are and what your family has been through.

We are permanently embedded in the minds of our local pharmacists because my water broke for CJ at the prescription counter. You can bet that made my son a near-celebrity with that local store. It is with great sadness that I report that now, five years later, that pharmacy has since gone out of business. My only options now are the large chain pharmacies. And boy, do I miss my little local guys.

Yes, progress has its costs. But some new innovations have come around that can be a mom's best friend. My new favorite ally in this parenting business is the internet grocery shopping service. These days, unless you live in a very rural area, chances are there is a service available to you. Electronics gadget fan that I am, even I was a bit skeptical at first. And I do have fun—yes, I said fun, and you'll learn more about that in chapter 11—at the grocery store with my kids, so I was in no hurry to try these services out. I admit, if you have to be very careful with your food budget, these services can be more expensive than your regular source for groceries. There are times, however, when they are worth their weight in gold.

Find one and sign on. Learn the site. Set up all the purchasing information so you are ready to go. Do one shopping experience. Many of these sites allow you to create personalized lists, and I highly recommend you take the time to do this now. Go through the entire process at your leisure so you are familiar with it. You now have an important resource when your two-year-old has a fever of 102 degrees and your newborn is running out of formula and diapers. When you are sick but your family's appetite is still very healthy. Any of those unavoidable moments when it just makes bad sense to take anyone into a grocery store.

You may be surprised, as I was, to see that a full week's worth of groceries is equal to or even less than your traditional source because there is no impulse buying. Your five-year-old can't talk you into Chocolate Frosted Sugar Balls on the internet. And your thighs may be pleased to know that it's much easier to pass up the Mint Milano cookies on the monitor than in the store aisle.

You don't need to become an internet grocery shopper every week to take advantage of this convenience. And it costs nothing to get yourself set up. You just need to be ready for when the call to "battlestations" comes your way.

The Bigger Issue of Health

All of these things represent good combat skills. But we can't ignore the bigger issue here: We, as parents, spend our days smack in the middle of a kaleidoscope of viruses. We would be doing ourselves a huge disservice if we didn't spend some time looking at what might keep us from getting sick in the first place.

It's the old flight attendant speech metaphor: Place your own oxygen mask on before you help your child. You'll hear me get on the self-care soapbox more than once in this book. Recognizing that we live in a germ farm is the first step in knowing that we need to take extra steps to keep our bodies combat ready. That means defining lunch as something other than peanut butter and jelly crusts eaten over the sink. (Don't believe a word of that old myth about food eaten over the sink not having calories—the fact that it has no nutrients might be closer to the truth!) Take a good long look at what you eat and you might find it rather disturbing.

> Recognizing that we live in a germ farm is the first step in knowing that we need to take extra steps to keep our bodies combat ready.

There's a good side to this. I don't know what your experience was, but I found it really tough to eat well as a working mom. The lure of the drive-thru was powerful when I was always so pressed for time. As moms at home, we can actually have *time* to cook. Even if it's just that we finally turned on that breadmaker Aunt Ethel gave us two Christmases ago. Granted, cooking with small children attached to your shins is a special skill, but you can learn how.

Right here is a good place to sing the praises of plastic picnic knives. I was amazed at how much fun one toddler can have with a piece of celery and a plastic picnic knife. They're not sharp enough to cut little fingers, but you can saw away at a stalk of celery with amazing vigor with one of those things. And—viola!—you have cooperative little cooks. Or at least cooks not reaching for the steak knives while you are trying to throw a chicken in the oven.

Part of keeping house is planning what and how your family eats. Some women can do this on the fly, but I need to have everything planned out. It makes grocery shopping easier, because I know what to buy and I'm less likely to find myself without the necessary ingredients. Two minutes in the cookbook section of the local bookstore gave me a host of resources, and I subscribed to *Prevention* magazine, which has dozens of healthy recipes.

You need to temper your information, though, when you have small kids. Once, I took two hours to make this delicious-sounding, nutrition-packed homemade macaroni and cheese recipe. It smelled wonderful. It even looked like the picture in the cookbook. I was bursting with pride as I set it on the lunch table.

You experienced moms are laughing right now, because I bet you know what happened: My kids turned up their noses faster than I could blink. My homemade wonder didn't look *one bit* like the stuff that comes out of the blue box. No amount of convincing that some forms of real cheese aren't day-glo orange succeeded.

You have to adapt. I don't know too many toddlers itching to try Swiss chard. What's more, I have found that many of the healthiest recipes just plain take more time than I can commit to cooking. No matter how good it is for you, I just don't have the time to make yogurt cheese. I barely have time to separate eggs most days. So I glean what works for my family and leave the hard-core-organic-gourmet stuff for some other time in my life.

Yes, We Have to Talk About Exercise

And then there's exercise.

I, of all people, have a powerful incentive to keep my body healthy. Not one member of my family has lived past seventy-five. I have now lost both parents to heart attacks. I am walking around with a loaded set of genes cocked and aimed straight at my life span.

All this meant nothing in motivating me to sign up for an aerobics class.

It wasn't until I began to understand the psychological and physiological aspects of exercise that I found anything that even smelled like motivation. Exercise does good things for your mind as well as your body. It even helps your hormones (for moody me, this was the deciding factor). I had to try several forms of exercise until I found something that fit. For me, slow-moving, resistance-based exercises like weight training and pilates give me the sensations of a healthy body that I need to stay motivated. They don't kill my muscles and my spirit like aerobics did, and can be done within ten feet of a small child. (Ever try keeping a toddler off a Nordic Track? It's nearly impossible!) Videos are fine, and I do use them, but for me nothing replaces the commitment of taking a class. Plunking down my hard-earned cash forces me to get into that class no matter how I feel.

There's a side issue here that many moms wrestle with. I take a class once a week at a local health center. With babysitting. Notice I didn't say "ideal child care." It's not. It's secure and clean, but it's not at the standard I'd set for full-time day care. Some days there are an awful lot of children in there. I'm sure some colds and flus (and worse) have come into our home from all those little hands and noses. But I have come to the decision that it is an acceptable trade-off. I believe it's very, very important to recognize that there are times when my welfare as a woman and a wife are balanced against that of my children.

For a long time, this felt selfish to me. I wrestled with the self-sacrificing idol of motherhood I'd known. Then I remembered that God slates my loyalties to him first, then to my husband, then to my children. If I do not care for the body God gave me, is that good stewardship? If I allow my physiology to get wacky from hormones or stress, am I serving my husband and family well? And, for me, if I do not take steps to overcome my cardiac risks, how dire are the costs?

If you are wrestling with the "second best" of letting someone else care for your children while you care for yourself—emotionally or physically—at the gym or the church's moms' group or even weekly worship, I hereby bestow on you a Chief Home Officer's Executive Privilege to put yourself first. It's not selfish to accept the minor costs of taking care of yourself. It's actually a valuable model to teach your children. While it may shred your heart to peel your crying eighteen-month-old off your legs so you can attend a class or a meeting, *believe me* when I say it is best for both of you (and I've shredded my heart dozens of times).

Trust yourself. Don't be foolish or reckless, but don't let their emotional *wants* hold your *needs* hostage. If it's really damaging or unsafe, you *will* know. Your gut will tell you loud and clear. But don't let the minor stuff— no matter how they wail or you cringe—keep you from taking care of your body. Your children will not end up in therapy as a result of an hour in an imperfect child care setting.

What may put them in therapy, however, is the day-in-day-out with a mom over the edge. Any glance at today's papers will give you heart-wrenching accounts of the consequences of moms over the edge.

At-home motherhood is a time to take your health seriously. The tools of our trade are inside our skin. Our healthy bodies and healthy attitudes are what allow us to be good mothers. They are our best defenses against the terrors and challenges of child raising. No one runs marathons on impulse—they train and take care of themselves. It's part of recognizing your executive value.

Remember your executive status. Companies take out millions of dollars in life insurance policies on their CEOs because they know how irreplaceable they are and the havoc wrought upon their organizations when an executive is gone. Really savvy executives craft transition policies for handing over power to someone new—temporarily or forever—ahead of time. We should take our cue from them. How much more do our families depend upon us?

The time you spend preparing for illness to strike your home is time well spent. The time you spend beating yourself up about illness finally getting in the door is time poorly wasted. It's coming whether you bleach your countertops everyday or not. So arm yourself with a healthy dose of perspective and preparation.

Personal Reflections

1. WHAT are your options if you are too sick to care for your children? Have you thought them through in advance? Take some time to prepare you and your household for the inevitable sick days that are coming your way.

2. WHAT about parenting has been "just plain awful" for you? What did you learn by getting through it? How could this affect how you handle crises or unpleasantness now?

3. HONESTLY evaluate how well you take care of yourself. How is your diet? Do you get regular exercise? What are the health risks you might be ignoring? Try to identify three things you can do in the next two weeks to improve your health.

Managing Your Staff:
Oh, Those Tiny Employees

IT'S JUST US.

Us, and them, and a whole lot of hours.

Hours in the middle of the night; hours stretching into summer's hot, sticky afternoons; hours on the tenth day of nonstop rain. Hours.

Time. Parenting is a lot about filling time. Filling it with good things, useful things. Silly and serious things. As a new parent, it is about looking at time in a whole new way. The bottom line is, time isn't yours anymore. Your time is no longer your own. You share it. And that little person doesn't exactly have the same interests and needs as you.

When my first was born, I found this shift particularly difficult. I was a time-manager. I conquered time to my advantage. Now, it felt like time had me over a barrel. Not enough time in many ways, too much in countless others. It took twenty minutes just to get out to the car to go anywhere. Run an errand? Ha! Dropping off film at the drugstore took almost the whole morning. Being on time for anything? Nearly impossible. The well-groomed control-freak in me was coming undone weeks before the end of my first maternity leave. And I did not go quietly. I did not acquiesce gracefully to my new role. I fought it kicking and screaming until my frustration level choked me.

Why? Because I felt like I was no longer in charge. That wasn't true, of course, but it was an emotional reaction. The truth was I was still in charge; I just had new needs to meet that were wildly different from what I had known. Being in charge means you *plan* for it to take twenty minutes to get yourself and your offspring out the door, not kick yourself into hysteria because you can't get out the door in ten minutes. Your authority hasn't changed, just the operating procedures.

The Danger of Winging It

Yes, you may have lost a great deal of your spontaneity, but you now have a crash course in scheduling and planning. Time is as much your friend as your enemy. For some children, some babies, "winging it" comes naturally. They can just go along for the ride in whatever you need to do. The fact that you just carry them around works in your favor (if your children are not old enough to either walk or object, you'll soon long for the days when it was just a matter of lugging the baby carrier around). Even that portability, though, can't override a nap schedule or a sensitive child's temperament on a permanent basis. Predictability helps young children cope. Sooner or later, each of us learns that schedule and routine are not words to describe a rut; they're words that describe a framework.

You *are* in charge. Most times you know what's best for your kids. If you're looking for permission to do things your kids hate you for, I'll be the first one to give it to you. The time your child insists he doesn't need a nap is often the time he most needs one. Sixty-eight Oreos does *not* constitute a lunch, no matter how many times it is requested. And if you say your child is too tired to go to the park, then she *is* too tired to go to the park. Period. Chief Home Officers know authority is no popularity contest. Even though I often listen to my children and try to remain flexible, I regularly pull rank. I remember that I was here first, I have their well-being at heart, and it is my job to plan, their job is to follow.

When I hear wails of protest from my troops, I love to lay blame on Big Bad Mommy School, that dark and dangerous place where all mothers learn such horrors as the virtues of vegetables, baths, curfews, naps, and candy restrictions. A mother friend of mine created this wonderful scapegoat and I use it frequently. I graduated magna cum laude from Big Bad Mommy School. I gave the valedictorian address. Mommies across America subscribe to its rules of conduct. And now that she's nine, Amanda has just about figured out that it doesn't really exist. Almost.

Especially when I had my second, I learned to make friends with my constraints. I learned that planned time made for an easier day. I won't make the assumption that what works for me works for everyone, but I will relay what we worked out in the hopes that you can glean something of use for your family.

As I related in chapter 3, we needed to stay busy to stay sane when I first came home. To get out and remind ourselves we were members of the human race. The trick became to find a level of activity that kept Amanda and I happy but wasn't too much for sensitive baby Christopher. I ended up breaking up the day into manageable "chunks." We slowly came to the realization that we could do well with three chunks: morning, midday, and afternoon.

We started by setting a morning routine. Even when I had been up all night with colicky Christopher, giving some framework to our mornings helped us keep it all together. I chose to anchor our routine to Amanda's favorite PBS morning show. For some reason, preschoolers can handle time concepts when wrapped around TV shows (yes, I know, this doesn't speak well of our culture, but you've got to work with what you've been given). So I looked at the broadcast time for Amanda's favorite show and divided up the morning into things that needed to be done before the show could be watched and what could be done afterward. I packaged these tasks with a mind to what CJ was doing at about that time so we could take advantage of coordination.

Such two-fisted thinking meant that Amanda and I ate breakfast together most mornings, snatching a bit of "just us" time while CJ slept. We tried to do things in the same order every morning. Amanda put up less of a fight getting dressed if she knew it came every day after TV. All three of us tried to get ourselves out somewhere each morning by around 10:30, when CJ woke up from his morning nap. And so it went throughout our day.

Another helpful trick was to set certain days for certain things. Tuesday mornings were for the library. Fridays were our days for playdates. Setting playdate days kept her from hounding me all week "Can I have a friend over?" If you don't have a child over four, you will not yet understand the particular agony of this repeated request. Any child from ages five to thirteen will tell you that life is just plain insufferable if they don't have a friend over every waking minute. A designated day helped everyone keep their cool and show a semblance of patience.

This scheduling is harder than just sorting it out in your own head. Like most four-year-olds, Amanda had a paper-thin grasp of time. "Not now" or "in a minute" or "on Thursday" meant nothing to her. She lived only in the here and now. I could not find ways to explain to her that we couldn't go to the park eight times a day or that lunch wasn't for another hour or that preschool was on Tuesday, not today. One day, in desperation, I began to draw her pictures. I made seven rectangles for the days of the week. I began to draw in the parts of our week that were fixed—preschool, etc. Looking at her, I could see the little light bulb go off inside her head. Amanda had to *see* time. She is still a visual learner—even at nine—so I had to discover ways to show her time.

We made little symbols for the things in her week: playdates, going to the library, grocery shopping, the park, swimming. She could grasp her week that way. She could look at those rectangles and understand that preschool was tomorrow, not today. Eventually I went to the office supply store and found one of those dry-erase schedule boards. I discovered that Colorforms (remember Colorforms?) stuck to dry erase boards. Now she could move a Colorforms circle through her rectangles to see where she was in her week.

And, perhaps more importantly, it forced us to sit down each Monday and plot out what the week would be like. I could see where the holes were in our schedule (yawning gaps of time just ripe for boredom and chaos) and find things to fill them—or to have on hand when down time just wasn't exciting enough. All this leads me to another basic truth of parenting: Planning is everything.

> I find I can let my planning requirements choke me, or I can learn to love them as my best defense against chaos.

You can blow off a plan if you decide that's best. Sometimes the most astounding fun comes in a spontaneous decision. On the other hand, you can rarely drum up a plan the instant it's needed. Parenting takes planning. Gobs and gobs of it. If you were never a manager with planning responsibilities, you've got to learn them now. It's that delightful, excruciating knife edge between the well-laid plan shot to ruins and the chaos of no plan at all. That's the daily existence we live as parents.

Plan your day. Plan your meals. Plan your fun. Hey, now that you have kids, you'll even have to plan your sex life (I told myself I wasn't going to get into that. . .). I find I can let my planning requirements choke me, or I can learn to love them as my best defense against chaos.

Tiny People Can Have Big Ideas

Having said all that, I feel I must temper all my praise of structure and authority with tones of mercy and respect. From such lessons comes another parenting truth: Respect your children. No, they are not little adults. But they are little people. Who are—can you believe it?—occasionally right. Children need to feel we've heard them, even if we still elect to pull rank. Some of the best parenting ideas I have had came from the answers to questioning my children, "Well, what do you think we should do now?"

There was a time, right when kindergarten started, when Amanda was rather unhappy. Part of that may have come from the fact that she was now five. In my experience, the terrible twos have nothing on the fearsome fives. It's another of those things you just have to gut through. Remember your parents sighing "it's just a stage"? They weren't too far off.

I could no longer cope with Amanda's constant unhappiness. It was tough going. Lots of crying. My normally bubbly girl was a lump of misery. No one—neither Jeff nor I nor her teachers—could find a path to success.

Finally, in an act of desperation, I flopped down beside her on her bed. I stop here and point out that I sat *beside* her. That sounds minor, but I have found that if you sit beside your child, you are talking *with* them. All too often if I sit in front of them, I fall into talking *at* them. We sat in silence. Eventually, I said something to the tune of "I can't figure out why you're so unhappy. Can you tell me what's wrong?"

After the usual list of five-year-old grievances, a tiny shred of evidence came out. "You and Christopher get to stay home all day," she said, "And I have to go to school."

This, I knew, was big stuff. "Tell me more," I said.

Parents, engrave *"Tell me more"* on your foreheads. When your child finally articulates a problem, remember to say this rather than to jump in with your idea of a solution. You'll be flabbergasted by what you learn.

Amanda felt that Christopher was getting the much better deal, staying home with Mom. I don't know if she thought we broke out the hot fudge sundaes the minute we put her on the bus or something, but she was convinced we were having loads of fun in her absence. It didn't matter how much fun kindergarten was if your little brother didn't have to go and you did. I had to respect that.

"Amanda," I offered after she had talked for a good long while, "you're learning one of the biggest lessons in life. The simple truth is you can't always do what you want." I let it sink in, in silence, for effect. This was the mother of all teachable moments.

"No," countered Amanda, screwing up her face in deep thought. "That's not the biggest lesson in life." She had her own idea of Life's Biggest Lesson. Somehow God gave me the grace to hush up and let her have the floor.

"The Biggest Lesson in Life," she pronounced, "is that you cannot give your baby brother back."

Oh my. Deep, deep stuff.

Big, hard issues for a five-year-old. We talked more about it, with my taking extra-extra care to show I respected her feelings. Just to see where it led I asked, "Well, what do you think would happen if we drove by the hospital and told them you were unhappy with your new little brother?"

I wasn't really surprised to learn she had thought through this already. "Nope," she replied, "he's much bigger now. They'd know. They wouldn't take him back." It somehow seemed to appease her, however, that I had even dared to ask such a question. In a few minutes we started talking about how cute he was at times. I told her—in precise detail—how CJ and I had spent our day while she was gone. I let her know having a colicky baby in the house has been hard on all of us, and that there were times even Mommy wished things were different.

Things got infinitely better after that. Not perfect, but better.

Most management books will tell you that often the best solutions come from the rank and file. This has been true of our family. At age three-and-a-half, Christopher was showing no signs of embracing this potty thing. He knew the mechanics, he knew the advantages, he just didn't want to get on board. I was frustrated beyond my capacity. Vacation Bible School was starting in three weeks and children needed to be trained to attend VBS. I was running VBS, so I really, really needed my kids attending. I had legions of people praying that CJ would catch on in time. Legions.

I got my answer, but it came in a much different package than I was expecting. We were sitting at the lunch table one afternoon, discussing as a family our "potty dilemma." Finally, the lessons of my brief parenting career actually sunk in for a moment and I turned to Amanda. "Can you think of some way to persuade CJ?" I asked, not really expecting anything useful.

That little light bulb went off in Amanda's head again. Amanda, smart girl that she was, utilized the most powerful persuasion she had: Amanda Day.

Amanda Day started as a way to give her some special time in the midst of dealing with all that hit our family since CJ was born. As a matter of fact, Amanda Day came about as a direct result of our Biggest Lesson in Life conversation. On Sundays, after church, Amanda got the afternoon to do the activity of her choice with the parent of her choice. Now it so happens we were having this little potty strategy summit on a Sunday. I watched Amanda carefully lay out the advantages of Amanda Day to her little brother. She finished up her little presentation with the newly-minted policy that "you can only have Amanda Day in *underwear*." So CJ, if he wanted CJ Day, had better get himself into those cool little training pants if he wanted in on the deal. Amanda also knew that the most exciting place in the world to Christopher was Dunkin' Donuts. So, for extra incentive, Amanda mentioned that the inaugural CJ Day could very possibly be a trip to Dunkin' Donuts. Ooooo. . .

As Jeff and I gaped in astonishment, CJ hopped off his chair and headed off in the direction of his bedroom—and, I hoped—to his underwear drawer. Amanda, with a smug-but-duly-earned grin, trotted off after him. She led him into the bathroom, took him through the drill (we could hear all this from the table), helped him pull on the training pants, and returned him prepped and ready to the dining room table.

> Who knew my answer to prayer would be a quick-witted grade-schooler wielding a chocolate-frosted-sprinkles doughnut?

It did not matter that we had not yet finished lunch. Nutrition was going to take a happy backseat to hygiene. Jeff and I jumped up from the table, loaded ourselves into the car, and headed straight to Dunkin' Donuts. And that, ladies, is how my son got potty trained. Who knew my answer to prayer would be a quick-witted grade-schooler wielding a chocolate-frosted-sprinkles doughnut?

Communicate, Communicate, Communicate

Even as toddlers, our children are smart. They are just as likely to be used by God as anyone over three feet tall. They're astounding. They *are* little people. Yet I am terribly bad at remembering this some days. I save all my clear thinking manners for the outside world and let my family see me with my hair down all too often. Sometimes we treat our families worse than any staff member we had as a member of the working world. Which brings me to yet another parenting truth: You must communicate your expectations. Your children can no sooner read your mind than your husband can the week before your anniversary. You need to tell them—clearly, calmly, in terms they can understand—what it is you need from them. Of course, that means you have to figure out what it is in advance, but hey, if it were easy we'd all be doing it, right?

Repetition and clarity can be your staunchest allies in this parenting business. Before we head anywhere where special behavior is needed, I repeat my expectations—ideally until the kids can say them with me. Children need to absorb rules in many different ways—my visual learners have taught me this. Our daily expectations are up on a chart in the kitchen. I tell them the chores, and they have chips on a pegboard that outline them as well. They know I expect them to turn each chore's chip over when they've completed their task.

When they were really little, I needed to live by the "divide and conquer" rule. At three and four, neither Amanda nor CJ could grasp what "clean your room" meant. They could however, get their little minds around a three-pronged approach. Instead of "clean your room," we used (1) straighten your bed, (2) animals and toys off the floor, and (3) clothes in the hamper. I have found that this three-part harmony works for a variety of different activities—and you'll hear more about that in particularly lethal situations in the next chapter.

The Magical Leverage of Cause and Effect

I am also a big believer in rewards and consequences. Try as I might (and I have tried mightily), I have been unable to help my young children grasp "because it's the right thing to do." It is rare to find such a value in adults, so I'm not ready to expect it of my children—even though I'll continue to teach it, hoping it sinks in someday. I do want my children to learn obedience, and there are some things that require absolute obedience in our house, but I don't want to wield that heavy hammer every moment.

I believe rewards have a golden place in child rearing. Rewards are not always tangible, but they must be meaningful. Rewards can be an extra goodie, the chance to stay up five minutes later (you'd be astounded at what an extra five minutes means to a child), or tokens which can be saved up for extra special things like a chance to go out for pie with Mom. Sometimes, a reward can be as clear-cut as explaining to the child that if we do the task now, we'll have more time to do something fun later. It's the magical leverage of cause and effect. Chores done throughout the week means we can do something fun on Sunday afternoon. Good behavior at the mall means everyone has a good time and we can come back soon. Peaceful backseat relations on a long car trip means we can stop at Dairy Queen next time we need gas.

Now I know there are parents who feel this strategy implants a "what's in it for me?" attitude in our children. But I ask you: Do you know any adults who go to work without a salary (not counting us at-home moms)? There's a fine line, a healthy place between recognizing the benefits and being a full-fledged mercenary.

The Power of Plan B

All of these day-to-day tactics are important, but there are larger issues that should drive how we raise our children. What is it you want your children to learn in life? This is a deep question and the answer isn't always obvious. It took me a few years of realizing what I valued in people (and children) to see where I was heading in raising my children. Once I put a name to it, however, my focus sharpened considerably and I was able to move forward with even more effectiveness and able to find new ways to instill the values I held dear.

About six years into my parenting—yes, it took that long—I recognized what I most yearned to teach my children. It was the ability to adapt. To cope. To roll with the punches. Resilience. The more I looked at what I admired in people, the more I realized how much I value that particular character trait. Hint: One easy way to see what you admire in people is to take a look at what drives you nuts in people. If something makes you bonkers, if something resurfaces time and again as your pet peeve, if it's your hot button; chances are its opposite is the thing you value.

I love *Star Trek*. I'd just love it if someone offered me a chance to spend a week—a day even—on the legendary *U.S.S. Enterprise* or it's more recent cousin, *Voyager.* Captains Kirk, Picard, and Janeway are heroes to me. And I have found more than a few life lessons amongst all the aliens and starships. As far as I'm concerned, the reason *Star Trek*'s ultimate villains, the Borg, conquered the galaxy was their *adaptability.* These evil robotic creatures "assimilated" every species in their path and were unstoppable because they could instantly adapt to any threat. If the clever Captain Janeway hit them with a new strain of photon torpedoes, they created a new defense before our hero could reload the next array.

Now, I am not aiming to have my children take over the galaxy. I do, however, want them to be as good as adapting as the Borg. I want them to embrace the philosophy imparted to me by one of my college professors: "Life," she would say, "is the ability to go to Plan B."

"Plan B." Those are crucial words at my house. We are The Plan B Family. The first response I want to hear when our family faces an obstacle is "Time to Go to Plan B." It is an excellent strategy for anyone—especially parents. We as parents had better be able to adapt all the way down to Plan G if needed. Adaptability has some wonderful by-products as well. Creativity, persistence, and problem-solving are all ingredients for a Plan B.

I knew I'd hit the mark on a recent vacation. Near the end of our very long drive to Florida, we were involved in a potentially serious accident. Not many of us can say we drove away from a head-on collision on the highway, but God protected our family and none of us were injured when an out-of-control vehicle spun into the front of our car. As soon as we had established that we were all okay, my youngest son echoed the family crisis motto: "Well, Mom," he said, "looks like we're going to have an adventure."

That's what we say at our house when trouble rears its ugly head. We reclaim our control and dub it an "adventure." Being locked out of the house in the dead of winter is an adventure—especially if it's snowing. Realizing in Maryland that I left my purse on my aunt's dining room table in Pennsylvania is a whopping big adventure (I admit I cried when that happened, but we found our way—and my purse—just the same). Finding out at the front gate that the zoo is closed is an adventure. Looking for the new waterpark when we left the directions at home is an adventure.

I'm not going to tell you that some of those adventures didn't turn out horribly. Some of them were just plain awful. Driving to Washington D.C. alone at night instead of in the daytime because my wayward purse added three hours to our trip was pretty awful. I was frightened about being in a new city with two children and no cell phone. We were heading to my brother's house, but I was leery of finding my way in the dark. I was upset at my irresponsibility, worried for my kids, and more than a little scared.

I will also tell you that halfway into that trip, as dusk fell and tensions rose, I had the joy of being comforted by my young son. The memory of him singing church songs to me as we headed down the highway far off our original timetable will stay forever. Preschool ditties about Noah's ark reminded me of God's mercy and sovereignty. There was an adventure hiding in that crisis, even *that* crisis. We made it just fine, and our whole family learned that God can protect us anywhere, anytime. When I think of that trip—which, incidentally, was a fabulous adventure for us that summer—I don't think of the Smithsonian or the Washington Monument, I think of Christopher's tiny voice ministering to me from the backseat. And I am deeply aware that Plan A would not have revealed that magic moment.

"What should we do now?" These are powerful questions for the Plan B Family. "How do we handle this?" "What kind of adventure will this turn out to be?" These are the questions I teach my children to ask in the face of obstacles. Obstacles that are as small as running out of NutriGrain Bars or as large as demolishing the family car. I believe they teach my children to think "What does God have in store for me to learn now?" instead of "That's it! I'm done for!"

It's the shift of a single word: not "problem," but "adventure." It's a powerful outlook on life.

The CEO's Lesson for the CHO

Such big lessons don't come in curriculums. You cannot download a five-point Vacation Bible School plan on resilience off the internet. These are lessons that come in a thousand tiny pieces over the course of young lives. What is it you want your children to learn? What character trait do you most value in adults? You don't have to create a vast life plan to put them to work. Often just giving it a name, a focus, is all you need. The emphasis blooms all on its own. And such thinking helps you as a mother to realize the all important fact that your profession is not about "doing" or "accomplishing." It's about building and being. Growing and molding. Those are wildly long-term, hopelessly invisible goals. If we're not looking carefully, the continual mundane of the everyday will drown them out. We will loose our purpose, our patience, and our perspective.

That's what separates CEOs from managers. Managers manage. CEOs provide vision, big picture thinking. Now we of course, as mothers, we are called upon for both.

Many of us could spout wonderful vision if someone else would just unload the dishwasher. So it is up to us to carve out time so the CHO can think like a CEO. Two hours at the local coffee shop with a pen, paper, and a mocha latte just might give you a glimpse at that target. CEOs are CEOs because they are trained that way, because they know the value of looking above the operational stuff to seek the vision. They carve out the time. They understand that it is worth the cost. So should CHOs.

I've just handed you an excuse not to vacuum this week—are you going to take me up on it? Show this page to your husband or whoever helps you watch the kids and plan an escape sometime soon. It might take you six hours—or six years—to stumble upon it, but it is worth the time.

It's also worth devoting prayer time to ask God to reveal it to you. In Psalm 32 God promises he'll instruct, teach, counsel, and watch over us. The vision he gives you will ring true and motivate you. It's God's True North offered specifically for your family.

It may even be different for your spouse than for you. Then, however, you can rejoice in the marvelous partnership of vision that is the product of your marriage. Your children get Double True North. And that's something you can set your compass on.

For the Lord gives wisdom, and from his mouth come knowledge and understanding. He holds victory in store for the upright, he is a shield to those whose walk is blameless, for he guards the course of the just and protects the way of his faithful ones.

Proverbs 2:6–8

Personal Reflections

1. How do you view your time now that you're at home? Is it friend or foe? Routine or rut? What

things might improve your feelings about how you spend your days?

2. ARE you happy with your level of activity? Would you say you have found a balance for the needs of each of your children? If not, what can you do to identify and achieve that balance?

3. WHEN is the last time a good solution to a sticky problem came from one of your children? When is the last time you even asked? If you haven't asked "What should we do now?" lately, commit yourself to doing it once this week.

4. Do you feel you communicate expectations clearly to your children? Where is the communication working? Where isn't it? How can you improve?

chapter 11

Advanced Labor Relations: Averting Strikes, Tantrums, and Other Disasters

DAY TO DAY parenting is the stuff of our lives. The endless cycles of diaper changes, homework, dishes, vacuuming, etc. With a little luck, we all find our rhythm about six months after entering this vast no-woman's-land we call "being at home."

Some situations, however, send us running for the hills. Challenges so daunting we tremble at the thought of them and wrack our brains for useful survival tips. Every mom dreads something different, but the ways to cope can be surprisingly universal. I'll share my most daunting Mom situations with you, in the hopes that my solutions can trigger some of your own. My killer challenges were (1) grocery shopping, (2) long car trips, and (3) summer vacation. The summer vacation issue also pertains to that dreaded first few months without child care. In other words, whatever set of circumstances thrust you into full-time child coexistence. Especially mom-child-infant coexistence.

I pondered what it was that these situations had in common. My theory is that each of these finds us—or our kids—in an environment for which we are not yet suited. Parents are not yet suited to be surrounded full-time by attention-gobbling children. Toddlers and school-age children are not yet suited to leisurely stroll the grocery aisles in search of the best whole-wheat muffin mix. I have yet to meet anyone in the parent/child continuum who came readily equipped for a long car drive. My husband is an automobile aficionado and he drives for fun. Drive? For *fun?* You mean like not *on the way* to somewhere? That one's lost on me.

In other words, each of these situations pits us against the elements. They are circumstances ripe for chaos. What are our weapons against the ravages of such hostile environments? Creativity, planning, and humor.

You Are How You Think

We have entered the realm of advanced Mommy tactics. Challenges above and beyond the ordinary would send a lesser woman running. But we can't run anymore than we can live without diapers or magically transport ourselves to a long-distance destination. If we were sensible, rational people, we would run for the hills and avoid these disaster-prone situations at all costs. But sensible and rational are not adjectives frequently associated with small children.

We need the stealth weapon of all Mommydom: The Attitude Shift.

We set the tone, folks. If we dread it, you can bet our children will dread it too. My offspring didn't learn their bone-deep fear of the dentist out of thin air. They learned it from me. I taught them, in a million invisible ways, how much the dentist is to be feared. And I'm teaching them, oh so slowly, that I can be wrong. I'm not smiling about crown work yet, but I'm trying.

So if we decide the long driving trip will be a nightmare on wheels, you can bet it will be. On the other hand, if we decide it's going to be a rolling carnival of adventure, chances are it will be. More than any other variable, it is my attitude that calls the shots. That's real power, ladies. Real power laden with some serious responsibility.

The attitude shift can transform nearly any moment, large or small. There are times when it will simply mean life gets a tad smoother. When an opportunity for horn-locking gets bypassed. The quintessential "spoonful of sugar" of Mary Poppins' fame.

Now and then, you will discover as much magic as that umbrella-toting mystical nanny Ms. Poppins when you apply your attitude shift. There are times when a spur of the moment idea turns a dangerous moment into a dandy one. I experienced this just recently at a local music festival.

Music festivals generally involving sitting and listening. Each year we think this will be great fun for the kids and each year we are wrong (when do you think we'll catch on?). Yet it is something we enjoy, and when the weather is beautiful, this outdoor festival is truly a delight. Every year the same scenario rears its head: Jeff and I find some musical group that really peaks our interest, and we spread a blanket out to hear their whole set. Even though this year we brought a book for Amanda and CJ's Gameboy (something I thought I'd never own but have now dubbed "Electronic Patience"), they would not allow us to sit and listen. Actually, Christopher was hap-

> *I've discovered that my attitude shapes my children's behavior. More than any other variable, it is my attitude that calls the shots.*

pily marching Ms. Pacman through her steps with the volume turned off, but Amanda, on the other hand, was bored to near tears. Her book failed to hold her interest, subverted by the large ice cream cone that had just passed by on the hand of some lucky child.

Things were getting testy. I wanted her to stop whining so I could listen, she wanted to get out of the boring grown-up place and go get some ice cream. Horn-lock. Yes! No! Yes! No! Sit down! I'm bored! You get the picture.

Boarding school was starting to look pretty attractive until I remembered that an attitude shift was what was called for. In a spontaneous thought, I pulled out the small notebook I always carry with me (writer's habit) and wrote "One."

I handed her the pen and told her we were writing a story, and the next word was up to her. You could just watch the gears turn (it helped that I handed her my "good" pen—the one I use for writing and signing books). Here is what came out of our game:

> One Love is Harold's only cheese shop. Cheese was smelly before feet trampled on it, but it never squished between toes much. It was special because this purple striped cheese's holes produced shoes perfectly. Harold's customers were devoted pickles and carrots. "Shoes, $1."

Don't you just love it? It was the most fun for the least amount of noise I have ever had. Amanda and I shared our love of story, I could still listen to the music, and I have this wonderful tiny tale to keep forever. We could have gone on for at least an hour, but the music set had stopped and it was—fantastically enough—time to get ice cream. Now instead of a grit-toothed discipline disaster, I have a wonderful memory and a new game to play whenever we're stuck waiting for something. That's the power of attitude shift.

Attitude Shift is your best weapon against the really big stuff too. Remember that Washington D.C. car trip from the last chapter? Seventeen hundred miles, three destinations, one parent, two kids, one minivan, 18,000 paper towels. My friends thought I was completely out of my mind. It was a trip I really wanted to take, a visit to my brother and some recently moved friends that were dear to Amanda and myself, and not a trip that Jeff could realistically take with us.

Now, I knew from the first moment I made this courageous decision that we were bumping up against the impossible. It was going to take some serious coping strategies to get us through this trip in one piece, much less enjoy ourselves. So I kicked my planning glands into high gear and gave this adventure the attention of a war campaign. It was a war. I was Mom against Chaos.

What was the most important decision I made? It was *that this was going to be fun.* Pure and simple. Sounds simple too. It is. Most important truths in life are. Thirteen hours alone in a van with two small kids *can* be fun.

No, really.

The Amazing Three-Step Car Fun Program

Don't put this book down and walk away shaking your head because of what happened the last time you tried to get farther than the county border with your kids, come back here and shift your attitude. It can be fun. There's just one small catch.

You have to *make* it fun. I'll walk you though the process we used, and you can scoop up what might work that special magic for your family.

Step 1: Divide and Conquer

I took a serious look at my family's attention span. It is different in different settings, so I focused in on what they could handle comfortably in the car. For us, with Amanda at age eight and CJ at age four, it was about one hour. My children, through their own, God-given personalities, are really good car-trip kids. They can go one hour without too many adjustments. I figured, then, that with the proper guidance and distractions, they could do two hours. I reinforced my thinking with a quick check with AAA, who informed me that the average adult can drive safely for about two hours at a time. Two hours became our measuring stick. I took my trip and divided it up into two hour segments. For this particular trip, that meant sixteen different time-chunks to be managed. For you it may be smaller—and you may just decide that a trip as long as we took is simply out of the question for your kids right now. That's a valid, useful decision.

I needed for my children to understand those divisions too. I knew that simply watching a clock or an odometer wouldn't be enough for them to see where they were in the journey. So I found a US map on the internet and printed out four copies (one for each day), using different regions for the different legs of our trip. Incidentally, it was Chicago to New Jersey to Washington DC to Chicago. Using a marker, I mapped out each day's eight hour journey into eight segments with circles. I numbered them 1–8. As we hit each segment, I announced it to the kids and they colored the circle in. When we hit number two, they knew there were two more segments before lunch time. I like to think it helped keep the dreaded "are we there yet?"s to a minimum.

Step 2: Distract

Each two-hour chunk needed to have a variety of fun, adventure-prone things to do inside the tiny confines of a minivan. We needed ammunition against the repetition of the miles and close quarters. I decided to attach three things to each two-hour chunk: (1) refreshment, (2) amusement, and (3) occupation. They sound closely related, but I chose things with those specific goals in mind.

Refreshment

For refreshment, I filled two boxes with two different kinds of car-friendly snacks. One box had food-type, something-close-to nutritious snacks such as granola bars, grapes, those tiny boxes of raisins, fruit snacks, little bags of peanuts, etc. I have an adult sister-in-law who swears that car trips are precisely why Cheez-Wiz was invented. I'm not proposing you hand your four year old a can of the stuff and kiss your upholstery goodbye, but it does get your brain thinking about what might be fun to eat. One of your best friends in this selection is novelty. Things you wouldn't normally let your children eat always spell fun. And, in my opinion, part of what makes a vacation a vacation.

Box two took this strategy a bit further. Box two contained sweets and treats, carefully picked for long-lasting effect. Things that take a long time to eat. This is why *I* swear the Tootsie-pop was invented. The box included licorice, tootsie rolls, little bags of M&M's, etc. Some of each child's absolute favorites (edited for mess factors) and a few things they'd never seen before.

I put the boxes out of reach in the back of the van. At every two-hour stop, we all got out of the car, stretched our legs, and each child chose one item from each box. I might add, however, that Mom had her own box. I didn't realize until far into the trip how important the physical act of getting out of the car was—even with all that entails for small ones with car seats. Fresh air is incredibly important. So, even though it was March, we got out at every stop, and once every hour (sort of our "we're halfway to the next stop" ritual), we rolled down all the windows and let new air in for ten seconds. It became almost a game and helped tremendously to break up the monotony.

Amusement

Now for goal number 2: amusement. This was our fun factor for each leg of the journey. With a few trips to the dollar store and other such places, I collected sixteen small but entertaining toys for the children. Things like wind up cars, tiny bottles of bubbles, little stuffed animals, and glow sticks (these are wonderful for that last hour of the trip when the sun is going down). This may seem like an obvious strategy, but here's the important point: I wrapped them. Not in gift paper, but in numbered paper lunch bags. That way I could control who got what when ("How come CJ got a hopping frog and I didn't?"), what order they came in, and portion size. I put all these bags, in order, marked for each child, in another box in the back. Yes, I could have just handed it to them, but it added another small element of fun for them to search through the box for their next bag. In a fortunate act of forethought I remembered to include a basket for each child to collect their prizes in over the trip. Half of the entertainment for me was listening to how the children would concoct plays and stories that wove the toys together. How the helicopter from hour three became the rescue vehicle for the doll from hour five. Yes, there were squabbles, but the fun I saw in their interaction often outweighed the tough spots.

Occupation

Goal number 3, "occupy" had it's own box too. These contained as large a collection of books on tape as my library card (combined with Amanda's for maximum volume) would allow. You haven't lived until you've recited "Sheep in a Jeep" from repetition-induced memory as you're barreling down the New Jersey Turnpike. It also contained two workbooks, age appropriate for Amanda and CJ.

The end result was a tiny Christmas at each stop. We'd all pile out of the car and open up the boxes to choose snacks, drinks, prizes, tapes, and activities. I am here to tell you we had an absolute blast. Yes, it took hours to pull all that together. Yes, it required additional effort on top of all the other massive details of such a trip. Was it worth it? Absolutely. Do my kids dread long car trips now? Not a bit. They think they're cool. And that is worth ten times its weight in Cheez-Wiz.

Step 3: Reward

Even with all the goodies I'd inserted, this trip was no small feat. And there were times where it required patience and other virtues not often associated with small children. I let Amanda and CJ know over and over how much fun I was having (and was only lying part of the time!), how much I appreciated their behavior, and how they were special children for showing me they could do this. And—of paramount importance—I booked us into a hotel with a swimming pool so when we arrived at our destination they had something extra-special to look forward to. Mom looked forward to the hot-tub after a long day's drive too.

Pre-Requisite to Steps 1-3: Prayer

Especially if you are going this alone without the benefit of a second adult, you need prayer. I needed to know this entire trip, from planning to the final turn into our driveway, was covered in prayer. I had people praying for our safety, for my creativity, for our lodging, for my alertness, for patience on everyone's part, and for what my Aunt Patsy refers to as "traveling mercies." Traveling mercies are those tiny, unplannable things that ensure your safety and pleasure. The extra-wonderful waitress. The fact that I left my purse in Aunt Patsy's dining room rather than at a roadside diner where it would have disappeared forever. The Dunkin' Donuts we spied at just the right moment. Noticing that exit sign just in time not to miss the turn-off. Over and over God gave me opportunities to show our children how he had blessed our trip. When things got sticky, we had faith that God hadn't left us at the last exit. I truly believe that it was this atmosphere that enabled Christopher to minister to me as we hauled down the turnpike so very late for our destination. He knew God was in the car with us because God had shown us in a zillion ways over the miles.

Am I a supermom consummate planner? Not really. I'll be the first to admit that fear spurred this planning as much as any higher motive. Fear that we'd all be miserable. Fear that my "adventurous spirit" was actually naive stupidity. I pleaded with God for creativity and insight as I led my family. He answered. There's no "S" on my chest, just a compassionate Christ in my heart. A savior who wanted my family to have fun and learn as much as I did. Who knew the value of the relationships I was trying to nurture in this trip. As it ended up, I became infinitely grateful for the visit to my Aunt Patsy, because my own mother died just three months later and Aunt Patsy has become a precious link to that part of my family. God enabled me to grow closer to my brother and aunt because he knew in a few short months I would need them tremendously. And that was the best—and most unexpected—lesson of all from my trip.

Paper, Plastic, or Pandemonium?

Now, next to a cross-country trek, a run to the grocery store may look easy, but any parent will tell you it's not. You lose any sense of novelty in something you must do week after week. There's not a lot of fun associated with keeping the fridge stocked. While the strategies are decidedly similar, this is a situation where attitude is everything.

People look at me sideways when I tell them I enjoy grocery shopping with my children. Most parents simply chalk it up to a necessary torture and muck through it. Some women I know simply avoid it by going when Dad can watch the kids (or better yet, I know families where Dad does the shopping—wow!). As far as I'm concerned, my time away from my children is far too precious to spend it in the grocery aisles. My only alternative, as I saw it, was to find a way to make it not only palatable, but hopefully enjoyable.

> As far as I'm concerned, my time away from my children is far too precious to spend it in the grocery aisles.

It's easier than you might think. The same three strategies of divide, distract, and reward apply. Again, I thought about how much time my kids could stand in the grocery store and still keep their cool. Honestly, it was a lot less than the car: I figured on twenty minutes.

As near as I could tell, my average grocery trip clocked in at one and a half hours. That meant I needed to find ways to break up my trip into three manageable time chunks averaging more like thirty minutes. The advent—at least in my community—of "upscale" grocery stores made this easy. My local chain added a coffeeshop corner with some tables and chairs. They also added some adorable (albeit lethal) kid-size shopping carts and a pleasant public bathroom. Yes, I did notice some items were more expensive, but if I kept an eye on the sales and still used coupons, the "upscale-ness" of the store didn't come through in my bill. And, as you'll learn later, these goodies more than paid for themselves in both cents and sanity.

The in-store cafe made Break Number One rather easy to recognize. If we went around 11:00, the first break could be for lunch. Not to mention Mom's beloved mocha latte fix (bound to put a better spin on any weekly chore!). I didn't have to explore very far to find fun lunches for my children inside the store. The chance to pick a Lunchable, something they normally do not get in school lunches or at home, is treated with the same envy as a trip to McDonald's. Even baby CJ, who for the first year had food from home, could appreciate the ability to share a cracker from the cool little package his sister had. Sure, it is an extra expense, but it is cheaper and a bit more nutritious than a trip through the golden arches. Our store even boasts freshly packaged sushi for me— where else would my children come to think of cucumbers as so very cool (except maybe Veggie Tales)? Most stores have salad bars now so if there's no sushi—or if the thought of raw fish turns your stomach—you have a good alternative. Our store has soup, pizza, and all kinds of goodies. My daughter tried her first tomato Florentine soup at those cafe tables. I doubt I'd have achieved an introduction to that food in any other setting. We permit ourselves to experiment in small, low cost ways. Essentially, we go out to lunch each week in the grocery store. What this accomplishes—the absolute essence of my plan—is to transform shopping from a "chore" to an "outing." It's a tiny attitude shift that works wonders.

Before the first break, my children are allowed to steer those tiny carts through the vegetable aisle and help me. I choose the produce section because it requires no label reading and contains mostly unbreakable items. My grocery list comes in two parts—produce and everything else. I have even drawn up picture lists for my kids so they can do most of the shopping themselves.

> The absolute essence of my plan was to transform shopping from a "chore" to an "outing."

For our first introduction into Mom's New and Improved Grocery Shopping, I made it completely fun: We checked out a copy of *The Very Hungry Caterpillar*, made a picture list of everything that caterpillar ate, and went shopping for it. This was complete fun—not a shred of chore-ishness in sight—even if it made for a rather odd lunch when we got home that afternoon. That one visit alone helped to shift my little ones' perception of the grocery store in enormous ways.

It's also wise to know your children's limitations when planning your assault on the aisles. I do not take a cart into the produce section—my hands are full just commandeering my little fleet of shoppers. We have fun and we learn. Yes, you heard me, the grocery store is a fabulous place for practical (and silly) life lessons. Thank you, Big Idea Productions, makers of Veggie Tales, my kids know their produce because of your talents. CJ learned counting and colors in the produce aisle. "What color is this apple?" "Can you put four lemons in the bag?" Amanda chooses whether we have red or green grapes this week. After we fill the little carts with the week's produce, we head for the Lunchables and indulge in Break Number One. This strategy works whether your children are small enough to ride or old enough to walk, because giving tiny ones a break out of the cart is important too.

After this lunch break we unload the little carts into one big one. I find this necessary because it is tiring to push even a little grocery cart no matter how cool they are. We've all seen them, those toddlers whining their way through aisle 14, their mothers telling them to "keep up" with their little carts, brothers ramming each other (or innocent onlookers wishing they'd brought their shin guards from soccer camp). Break One provides a natural place to end that portion of the fun.

The portion between Breaks One and Two requires attention and good behavior in order to get the fun part of Break Two. Here, in the aisles, is where you must put your creative mother hat on. There are a multitude of choices your children can make within the grocery aisles if you just look for them. Your children can see who spies Dad's favorite breakfast cereal first (believe me, there is no reading required for this!), choose what shape pasta gets used this week, get the number at the deli counter, decide what crackers get bought, etc. Here is also where I often let my children choose a canned good for the local food pantry (another important lesson).

Break two usually involves using the bathroom (most stores have finally caught on that patrons need to use a restroom often in the store and spruced them up for public use), and something small but fun like visiting the lobster tank. Yes, fun is to be found at the fish counter. The lobster tank is, for some reason, a source of endless entertainment for my children. Perhaps this is enhanced by the fact that I grew up in New England and have no fear of the spiny little creatures. I pick them up and handle them with almost as much glee as when I get to eat them. Now, I don't pick them up in the store, but my kids have seen live lobsters up close and are fascinated by them. The fish section staff, as they have come to know my children (believe me, people *notice* happy, behaved children in the grocery store!), play up to them. Some-one will invariably hoist a lobster out of the tank for them to inspect, offer them a slice of cheese, or just pay them the lovely compliment of remembering who they are by saying hello. When we reach Break Two, my children can select from a narrow list of rewards if—and only if—they've followed our rules for grocery store behavior. In my house these are no running, no taking something off the shelf without asking my approval first, and staying within sight. One infraction and you loose your chance to have a little cart. Two infractions and you loose your reward. Every time we enter the store I recite these rules—my children now recite them for me.

You can stretch this out as far as you want. In my store Christopher knows his favorite reward, a Hotwheels car (a whopping lot of incentive for $1.29) is in aisle 14. He learned number recognition lickety-split when he realized he could plot how many aisles were left until his reward. In our house, you are allowed to pick your reward at Break Two. This means, however, that you can only *hold* it. Never forget what just holding something means to a child—as adults we often hop straight to *having* something. Children, especially young ones, take glee in just *holding* something. I have also found that *holding* sweetened the *having* when you got that far. My children still need to behave clean through to the checkout line if they want to open it when we are done shopping. From Break Two until the checkout line, I still have the power (and often use it), to take the reward away if they misbe-haved. Sometimes only for five minutes, sometimes for good.

Like most consequences, you must be prepared for the massive objections the first time you enforce them. You may only need to do it once, but it will most likely be ugly. Be prepared to leave the store for the first couple of visits until you hit that nasty moment where your children face the consequences for the first time. You will lose that grocery trip, but your children will know—in no uncertain terms—that you mean business and your threats are not idle.

This "hold it, then have it" system has an added benefit: because the children were usually holding their rewards at the check out aisle, I have had very few checkout-line-candy wars. Unless they ask to have a piece of candy as their reward (something I allow occasionally—especially when the M&M's are calling my name), they already have something in their hot little hands so the lure of the sugar isn't very strong.

Once my kids got it in their heads that grocery shopping is fun, they became the source for new and even more creative rewards. One of the most surprising was "up and over." We own a minivan, so I pop the hatch to load the groceries in it. I usually have the third back seat folded down for added room. One day, Amanda and CJ asked if they could enter the car through the hatch, crawling "up and over" the seats to tumble happily into their places. Motherhood has taught me, thankfully, that sometimes it is a gift to say "yes" when you can't think of a good reason to say "no." After all, the hatch was already open and they had been good in the store. All it meant for me was one less door to open. It is a tiny thing and I cannot, in my grown up mind, understand the tremendous glee this holds for my children. But I'll be the first to capitalize on it. In all honesty, the sight of small, sneakered feet sticking straight up out of our middle seat underscored by happy giggles makes lugging those bags just a touch easier. When I let them scramble in first, they're usually done and buckled in by the time all the groceries are in the van.

If left to my own sensible devices, I could not have come up with such a treat in a thousand years. Rampant

> Motherhood has taught me, thankfully, that sometimes it is a gift to say "yes" when you can't think of a good reason to say "no."

silliness over mundane things is what makes children the gifts they are. As such, you will discover over the months (or in our case years) that if you practice the Pleiter brand of happy grocery shopping, you will probably never need to upgrade the strategies. Your children will do it for you. To your great amazement and delight.

These grocery shopping strategies will have two consequences. They will take more time in the grocery store—we now average about two hours a trip or more if we're having a whole lot of fun (it really does happen!). Yet, they are two fun, useful, hours—and that beats one and a half hours of drudgery hands down in my book. The addition of snacks and treats will also cost you slightly more money. You can decide in advance how much peace in the aisles is worth to you, and plan accordingly. If you can afford $10 extra dollars a week, then do lunch. If you have to be very careful with your grocery money, have a snack rather than lunch. You are in control. You can set the price limits. In our store, donuts are only $.50 and very popular.

Before you get up in arms about adding to your grocery budget, I'd like you to consider what I have discovered: It is more than likely your peace is paying for itself. Like any adults, moms simply make better choices when we are calm. You will have the opportunity to examine the better buy because you will not be spending all your energy controlling feisty children. And the way I figure it, our system greatly decreases the chances of Chocolate Frosted Sugar Bombs making their way secretly into our cart. Or Mom reaching for a box of Dove Bars in desperation (oh, surely this never happens to you?!?). Peace and planning work wonders for not only a mom, but her grocery budget as well.

Granted, it sounds complicated, but it's really not. Perhaps the most compelling evidence for its benefits is this: When summer comes, my daughter gets excited that she can finally come grocery shopping with CJ and me. Yes, you heard me, excited. My children actually are sad when they can't come with me. How often have you heard that?

Summertime, and the Living Ain't Easy

Now comes the mother of all parenting challenges: summer vacation. CJ's April birth thrust me into a scary new situation when he was first born. Within a month of his birth I would be facing a long, hot, day-care-exempt summer. Just Amanda, grumpy (and I mean *grumpy*, colicky, nocturnal, etc.) CJ, and me with nothing but long days to fill. I was flat out terrified. At day care, Amanda had everything a preschool girl could want. All summer long she had *just me*. As I explained before, I have learned the basic rhythm of filling a child's day, but summer still poses a considerable challenge. As a matter of fact, the older the kids get, the tougher that challenge becomes. Summer in our house is where the TV becomes a siren song, luring us into days of couch-laden inactivity if I'm not vigilant and careful. I have learned to apply Allie's rule of divide and distract here as well.

Take it one week at a time. It helps me to divide up my summer. I can't plan an entire summer break, but I can plan a week. When Amanda was about four it hit me that I needed some kind of framework, some kind of structure on which to hang my thoughts. Something that would kick my imagination into gear, spur us into activity, and help me seek out things to do. I sat down with a calendar for June, July, and August (I still do this every year and find it enormously helpful) and inked in the known quantities: travel, swimming lessons, Vacation Bible School, community events I knew about, and holidays. For us, summer runs between ten and twelve weeks each year.

I made a chart—a grid, if you will. Across the top were columns marked Theme, Books, Crafts, Food, Outings. Down the left hand side I listed each week of the summer. I began to think of basic, kid-friendly topics for each week. Nothing extraordinary—things like fish, stars, butterflies, farms, houses, trucks, etc. A glance around your child's room or his favorite books will help you here. Just the list seemed to be the first ingredient in my imagination. Just as writing out your goals—no matter how clear they may be inside your head—seems to magically instigate the process to make them happen, drafting this list each year always sparks my thoughts. As the weeks drew nearer to summer, I kept my eyes open for things to do related to these topics. Some were obvious—Goldfish crackers as one of the foods for "fish week," for example. Jell-O jigglers go a long way in this department—a cookie cutter for each week will take you quite far (and then you can cut bread with the same shapes for toast and sandwiches!). For "star week," I found a tiny observatory at a local college. I would have never even bothered to look if I hadn't been prompted by my weekly topic. Would I have purchased and tasted a star fruit on my own? Probably not. We have taken train rides—just three stops into a neighboring town for lunch and back again—for "train week" with extraordinary results. I have used the exhibits running at local museums as themes for weeks—you've got your outing built right in. The local zoo can serve for weeks on farms, birds, jungles, etc.

It doesn't take a dominant creativity gene to do this. Making the list a couple of weeks in advance seems to wake up your brain. Ask around, pour over family magazines, fire up your favorite internet search engine. For "house week," I invoked the age-old standard of driving to the appliance store to pick up two refrigerator boxes. I cut out doors, stuck them in the driveway with three large tins of washable poster paint, threw my kids into old clothes, and finished half a novel on the deck while my little developers created a subdivision in our driveway. The photo of three-year-old Christopher covered—and I mean *covered*—in paint is one I dearly treasure. The child is awash in color and glee. The only trouble came when

CJ, still coated in paint, chose to fill his diaper. It was the first time I changed a diaper on the driveway! Standing up! After they finished I just soaped them up and turned on the sprinkler. This, to a young child, rates right up there with Disney World. For double the fun—and twice the help—invite another summer-stricken mother over to join in. You might actually have a lengthy adult conversation while your little charges are in the cardboard construction business—and *that* is an absolute necessity during the summer.

The internet is a godsend in this endeavor. You can find coloring pictures, online games (Who would have known that a gas station has an online dot-to-dot car game for "truck week"?), a host of crafts, and other helps. The card catalog at your local library will send you home with a host of books on almost any topic you can think of (that's how our *Very Hungry Caterpillar* outing came about—don't you just love symbiosis?) Whether or not your kids pick up on the theme is almost irrelevant—its real strength is a planning tool for you.

Some years I have found we leave the structure behind by about the end of July. We have learned our summer rhythm, settled into our days, and don't need something prodding us on. Other years we've clung to it like a safety net. Like most good plans, it's there when you need it, and you can easily step away from it when you don't.

I didn't think it had much impact outside of my sanity until the second year. Around Memorial Day, Amanda walked up to me and said, "Mom, are we going to have fish week again this year?" It was not a moan as I would have expected; it was a request! Even though she'd never expressed any outright pleasure or approval of our theme weeks the previous year, they'd somehow made an impression on her. Anything positive your children *actually ask for* is worth its weight in Goldfish crackers!

Here, perhaps, is the greatest value in this strategy: I have found it helps both me and my children to *look forward* to summer. We have a delightful history of wonderful discoveries (and rainbow diaper changes) to draw from that generate a longing for what the new summer will bring. What a gift for your children to know that you're eager (okay, that may be a strong word in this case) for grade school or preschool to let out so you can explore the world together. They will sense it, believe me. I, once the most anxiety-stricken mother on planet earth, can guarantee this to you: The fear and trepidation of the first summer will fall away more each year until you can sincerely tell your children how much you're itching to spend the summer with them. Think about the precious, affirming message that sends.

Isn't that what God wants for us as parents?

Like our car trips, I have learned to cover my summer in prayer. Starting around April, when my usual how-am-I-going-to-survive-this-summer panic sets in (don't be fooled, it still does even after five years), I begin to pray. I pray for a right heart, for the attitude to look upon the summer as an opportunity, not an endurance test. That I will begin to yearn for the long, unhurried stretches of time with my children. For patience and creativity. For health and safety. Like the car trip, each summer I see the evidence of prayers answered and God working in my summer in ways I could not have begun to imagine.

This year, now that my children are both hitting grade school, I elected to take it a step further. For several months I had been feeling a tug to take the spiritual training of my children more seriously. To become more deliberate and proactive in teaching them God's truths rather than just seizing those teachable moments that erupt everyday. I'll admit the prospect made me a trifle anxious—adding another layer to our summer planning. And yet, as it is with most important things God has in mind for us, I could not shake the idea. Reluctantly, apprehensively, I took a deep breath and prayed that God would be blunt in showing me how to do this.

He was.

When I opened up my devotional reading for that day, I found myself staring at the Ten Commandments. Not just the familiar list of Thou Shalt Nots from Deuteronomy, but a verse I'd not seen before (Deut. 6:6–7). One that charges us to "teach these to your children." That's blunt. Giant-two-by-four-from-heaven-between-the-eyes blunt. Don't ever think God is required to be poetic and subtle. He has promised to give us guidance and counsel when we ask for it. If you need it spelled out for you in no uncertain terms, let him know. Think about it—your Creator knows how your brain is wired. He did the wiring. He is not likely to miss the ideal way to get his point across. Your job is to be looking for it and asking for it.

So even though I knew what the answer was going to be, I fished out my "Summer" file to see how many weeks summer vacation was this year. You guessed it; ten. No burning bush required; I got the message loud and clear.

As I began to pray for the wisdom to implement this little Divine Command, I took great joy in watching God lead me to the bookstore where I found marvelous books that translated the commandments into children's language. To ideas that matched topics to commandments— I don't think I'd have connected "honor thy mother and father" to family trees to a trip to the local arboretum on my own. Guess who's been learning God's truths alongside her children?

Attitude Overkill

The three situations I've just dealt with are good examples. Positive models of attitude. But I can't let this chapter go without taking a moment to talk about the dark side of Mom's 'Tude Patrol. Those things we think we can conquer with enough optimism but turned out to be just plain dumb of us to get into in the first place.

I excel at this. Sometimes I take all my knowledge of our family's strengths and weaknesses and throw it out the window. Why am I then surprised when things spiral out of control?

It harkens to the managerial legend of the executive who made a horrendous, multimillion dollar mistake. His company would pay dearly for his error in judgement, and this hard-working boss was distraught. With a heavy heart, he drafted his resignation letter, sure it would be demanded, certain he had to be punished for his bad decision. Without a word, he walked into his superior's office and handed him the single sheet of paper.

"What's this?" The CEO asked.

"My resignation," replied the executive.

"You can't resign now," countered the CEO. "We've just spent millions of dollars training you!"

How much better managers we would all be if we looked at our colossal errors as intensive training.

I decided one Sunday evening before school started that we'd take a trip to the local Ikea. This is a massive, inexpensive furniture store that is one of those places requiring stamina, strategy, and patience. Lines. Distraction. Sheer unadulterated volume. Tough going for adults, much less young children.

Ah, my persuasive brain argued, but it has some of the best, least expensive children's furniture around, and Amanda needed a desk for homework. School would be starting in a few days. Sunday evening would be the least busy time of the weekend, and it'd be *so helpful* to have Jeff with me. I rationalized and justified this thing into a nice, neat, box of denial.

In truth, this trip was a meltdown waiting to happen. Even though the store had a restaurant ("We can take a break for dinner," I told them), Sunday evening was no time to drive two children thirty minutes to a huge store to lug home a trunkfull of ready-to-assemble furniture. As I stood in our fourth line of the evening at 8:45 P.M., children whining, everyone tired, husband near the boiling point, I was still trying to put a "happy family outing spin" on everything.

It was a bad idea. It had been a bad idea from the first moment. Yes, a worthy goal, surrounded by good intentions, but a bad idea. Finally, God gave me the grace to look at my husband and say, "This was a mistake. This is everything you hate about shopping wrapped into one excruciating experience. I'm sorry."

There was no spoonful of sugar to make this medicine go down. No "attitude shift" would move this fiasco into an acceptable realm. Listing all the very worthy reasons why we needed to get this desk this day only made things worse. We had no business being there that late trying to accomplish all those things. We drove home in near silence. I bit my tongue each time I tried to justify things. I shut up and paid attention to my colossal error and tried to learn from it, because that is how visionary leaders learn. They fail, but they don't resign.

This chapter has been filled with challenges I felt I couldn't conquer on my own. What are yours? Have you stopped to think how they might, like our beleaguered executive friend, be opportunities for training in disguise? God cares about how you get through your daily life. He cares about carpools and being the room mother. He cares about day camp and swimming lessons. He cares about what your life is like on the inside and on the outside. God *is* in the details. And the dilemmas. Look for his presence and watch the wonder that unfolds in the most unlikely places. He's ready to invest in training you. And he won't let you resign either.

Personal Reflections

1. WHERE has your attitude colored your children's attitude for better or worse? When has it been your ally? When has it made things worse?

2. WHERE would "Divide, Distract, Reward" help in your family?

3. WHAT things keep you from planning solutions to your challenges? Time constraints? Lack of energy? Thinking of yourself as uncreative? What can you do to change things so you can be a better planning mother?

4. DOES your family have a self-invented game like "up and over"? What might make you say "no" to something so silly? How can you encourage yourself to say "yes"?

chapter 12

Downsizing Even in the
Best of Families

I BELIEVE IN the sovereignty of our Lord. I believe he can orchestrate events to create a level of provision that astounds us.

I also believe that there are times when he requires us to step out in faith even though we feel doomed. Sometimes, to grow in our faith, we must jump and learn that he will catch us. I have seen it in my own life. I would have never attempted being a stay-at-home mom if I'd simply looked at the impossible economic equation. I had to step out in faith. In my life, in countless others throughout time, God has blasted through the boundaries of common sense and logic to put land under the feet and food on the table of his people. For my family.

It would be nice if our lives read like a Hollywood screen epic. Yes, it happens some times, but certainly not all the time. Sometimes there are lessons that can only be learned when the walls *don't* come a-tumblin' down. We are left, standing outside of our own personal Jerichos, wondering how many more times we ought to be marching around. While in the last chapter you heard me exude the joys of God's bluntly apparent commands, there are times when he chooses to be the still, small hard-to-hear voice, not the pillar of fire.

There are few of us who will not one day face the reality of having to contribute once again to the family income. Conditions and needs change. Emergencies happen. Obstacles rear their ugly heads. Like our corporate counterparts, Chief Home Officers must sometimes face the realities of getting "downsized" for a season or for a decade. Like our corporate counterparts, we must look upon this as an opportunity to let God transform us again. Oh, but that's far easier said than done.

Downsized for a Season

This season fell on our family when Amanda was eight. It was not an error in judgement on our part, or poor planning, or any reflection of how sacrificial we were prepared to be in our family finances. It just *was*.

I felt broadsided. Kicked in my maternal gut. As I stared into the face of this fact, grieved and frightened, my faith trembled. Where was the God who passionately pulled me from the workforce, who grew me and pruned me to this marvelous new creation, who had astounded me for years with his provision and his protection?

Still there.

The answer was that he was still there. God had no more left me than he left Moses as he wandered the desert or Joseph as he sat in prison. It took weeks before I even thought to ask the question: Could God really be in my returning to work? It seemed impossible. I must have missed something somewhere. Surely God couldn't put this in his perfect plan for my family. Yes, it was only part-time work, and not just so our family could have the little "extras" in life, but even that felt like I was selling out. Letting my worldly needs rip me from my godly calling. It had to be wrong, to be a weakness. I agonized over it with the same intensity I agonized over leaving the workforce. Had my checkbook finally won out?

There may be instances where our panic to boost the bottom line really is a product of a consumer-fed lifestyle. Returning to work is not a situation to ever enter into lightly.

Then, there are instances where it is purely a fact of life. I firmly believe that into every family may fall the span of time when a working mom just *has to happen.* For me, the facts simply could not be denied. Issues needed to be faced. Important needs were going unmet. I looked at the situation with the same criteria I had made my initial decision: What is best for this family? Over and over the conclusion came that what was best for this family, what would create the smallest amount of upheaval, reduce stress, keep solid foundations, and provide stability for this family was for me to once again contribute to the family income. At least for a time.

I tried to be a good sport. Really, I did. I tried to remain thankful for the privilege I had of staying home for the crucial years. I would be lying if I said that I swallowed my resentment easily. Far from it. I went back to work kicking and screaming. More precisely, I went crying. My heart felt like it was made of cement as I sent word out to the fundraising community that I was once again looking for consulting contracts. If I was honest with my Lord, I raged at the position he had put me in. To have to do this after all that had transpired. I was angry. This was not fulfilling or contributing to the world around me; this was slavery to a paycheck. Budgetary imprisonment. I wanted to fight back against God. I was eager to wrestle with that angel even if it meant I would walk away with a limp.

My bitterness blinded me to the host of provisions God sent to ease my path. The neighbor who agreed to watch my son while I had meetings. The fact that I could find well-paying, consulting work where I had a considerable amount of control over my schedule. How it was so much easier to do this when Amanda was old enough to be in school full days. Colleagues who lent their hands in sending work my way. The plain, regrettable truth is that I could not see that God had not left my side. He was calling me to a reinventing of another kind, but I faithlessly ignored him. I angrily ignored him.

It is humbling to write this. It was not my finest hour as a child of God. You would think I'd have caught on. Truly, I had my share of faithful experiences from which to draw, plenty of chances to remember that the God who saw me through coming home hadn't fled the scene. I couldn't see the plan, so I couldn't believe it was there.

> Take one moment and entertain the thought that perhaps there is something astounding in his plan, but that it is currently out of sight.

If you are at this place, know this: God *has not left you.* He is right there by your side, waiting to show you what this new, uncharted season might hold for you and your family. Take one moment and entertain the thought that perhaps there is something astounding in his plan, though it may be currently out of sight. There may be something truly extraordinary beyond this place, or you may just have the opportunity to learn what it means to follow when you cannot see the way. Both are valid. Both are precious. Both are crucial to whatever transformation God has for you.

It is hard stuff. Just when you think you've got this parenting thing down, the rules change and you have to add a job to the mix. It is time to take yourself—and most likely your whole family—apart again and rearrange the pieces to fit the new setting. Take heart, oh seasoned executive, you have done this once before. Remember how scary it felt when you first jumped in the deep waters of being at home? This is just another patch of deep water. You can do it again.

Reinventing All Over Again

Where to start? Every woman's situation will be wildly different, but I do believe there are some key steps to surviving the CHO's downsizing. I'll walk you through my experience in the hopes that you can pull useful information for yourself.

Start with Facts

Chances are, if your family knows you need to reinsert a second income, you know the first important piece: How much money is needed. Jeff and I took a few weeks to work with our family budget, adjusting here, experimenting there; playing with the numbers to see just how small we could narrow that menacing gap between income and outflow. It was important that we looked at not only expenses, but savings, contingencies, college, and all the other pulls on a family's tight dollar. Sure, there was always the small hope that if we just ran that spread sheet *one more time,* the zeros would magically line up and our problem would disappear. Ah, but, it would solve nothing to kid ourselves. It was more healthy to look the problem in the eye than to pretend fiddling with numbers would change reality.

Pray, and Then Pray Some More

I prayed. And prayed and prayed. For wisdom and attitude. For boundless grace. For a sense of humor.

For easy money. Why not?

You know that saying that if you bring God a thimble, he'll fill it; and if you bring him a bucket, he'll fill that too? Well, I decided I was going to haul in a swimming pool. I specifically prayed that God would send one fundraising consulting client for one job with enough of a budget to fill the hole for the entire year. I figured it was a big problem, so it needed a gargantuan solution. After all, I had a pretty big God—and a pretty big hole.

It might have made for a more dramatic story, but that didn't happen.

I know why, now. This was one of those lessons God required me to learn an inch at a time. Receiving one sweeping, epic solution wouldn't teach me what I needed to learn. It would be like those fad liquid diets that drop all your weight in a few weeks—only to have it return ten-fold once you're off the liquid because you haven't changed any of your eating or exercise habits. Knowing me, I'd blow off any attempt at keeping the balance because it would be "just for this one time." I needed to learn how to do this on a semi-permanent scale because God had plans for me I had not even dreamed of (you'll hear about that later). Plans that would require me to have the balancing skills and priority focus that I could only learn over time.

But I didn't know that then. I was not happy that it was going to take a collection of efforts to keep our fiscal ship afloat. We were looking at two or three client projects throughout the year (but at least I could take the summer off and just work in the winter, spring, and fall). In a fit of optimism, we split the dollar gap in half for our first goal, hoping that by the end of the year the situation might have changed.

I looked at our nice, realistic, faithful plan. And then I cried more. I just didn't want to do this. And I suspected, perhaps, there was the lesson for me.

Weave a Safety Net

To keep my whining to a bearable minimum, I decided a little bit of earthly support might be in order. I chose a few close friends to share our situation with at first. For me, this was tremendously difficult. I, champion of motherhood, surprise candidate for the new-and-improved-stay-at-home-mom, was *caving*. Of course, that's not true. I was not caving on my principles; I was responding in the best way I could to a current—and hopefully temporary—family situation. But it felt like big, flashing, public failure. To tell myself over and over that it wasn't a failure wasn't really useful. It was more useful for me to face my irrational emotions and take steps to get over it.

Telling my first friend was a gut-wrenching experience. My going back to work meant I could no longer spend the morning each week I had treasured helping this particular friend with her writing career. Though I knew better, I worried that our relationship might not survive the drastic cut-back in time together. And these mornings were a tremendous pleasure for me. A beckoning eye into the writing career of which I had begun to quietly dream. I cried the entire way to her house.

I pulled myself together enough to ring her doorbell. She opened the door, said hello, and I made it all of four seconds before I burst into tears in her foyer. Wise woman that she was, she recognized the grieving for what it was, and comforted me. She supported my decision, for she knew the agonizing that had brought it about. I worked my way through the tight circle of friends until my confidence began to peek through and I could wrap my arms around the concept of going back to work. Each friend reminded me of how I had adapted before and could adapt again. God sent a tiny helping hint with each conversation. When I had tackled the first two or three tiny parts of this problem, God sent me more confidence and trust to tackle the next slightly bigger part.

Going back to work is as individual as coming home from work. Such a transition might come easily for you. You might even welcome it. There may be parts of your working world that you miss and would welcome back into your life. If we're really honest, there are some of us who have children so trying that the chance to do *anything* away from them on a regular basis is rather enticing. It's okay to admit that. Really. No truly honest mother is going to look down on you for that. We have all been there—even though the Betty Crocker in us thinks it's ugly to admit it. Your heart and your situation are unique to you and between you, your family, and God.

If you find, however, that its gut-wrenching nature catches you by surprise, cut yourself some slack. Recognize this for the hugely difficult transition that it is, and go as slow as you can manage it.

Remember God's Faithfulness

If you were a working mother before, you know the tight-wire act of day care, sick days, and job tensions. Here is a good place to remind yourself—every day—that you have done this before. Think back to those first frightening days at the end of your first maternity leave. Talk about fear! Recall what is was like to pull yourself from the "babymoon" of new motherhood and stand unsteadily on your feet back at the office. It takes a scary while before your brain stops telling you there is no way you can pull this off. It is, in fact, almost harder to return to working motherhood a second time because you have a full, weighty knowledge of it's rough spots.

> *Recognize going back to work for the hugely difficult transition that it is, and go as slow as you can manage it.*

Choose instead to temper that informed anxiety with the stability of experience. It may take awhile, but you will find a rhythm. When I returned to work after Amanda's birth (my first), it took about four or five months before the constant effort and tension settled down. Most importantly, remind yourself that you *did* find your feet, and that you *can* navigate these choppy waters until things calm down. Every working mother eventually hits her stride.

If you have not been a working mother, you have some extra adjusting to do. If you, like me, enjoyed a strong career and success, be prepared for a whopping undertow of conflicting responsibilities. Even if you have chosen to return to a job with nowhere near the level of responsibility you once had (a very good idea, by the way), this dual stress will feel like it's pulling you apart. I felt like I'd been strapped to one of those medieval torture devices that pulled a person's limbs in four directions. It is no longer possible, in most cases, for you to stay late and get the job done. To put in those star-employee hours. You will not be able to devote the energy to excel as you once did. Chances are you can be a good, solid, employee. It is more likely, however, that you must leave the employee of the month status to your husband and just be average (or perhaps less than average).

This was, for me, very hard to swallow. A new chance all over again to say goodbye to the work-related self esteem and rely solely on the heavenly inheritance and the honor and glory that come long after my earthly tenure.

It's a job. It's just a job. Oh, those were such hard words for me to swallow. I wasn't cut out for "just a job," I was a *career* woman. Whether I chose to go back to work at the local coffee shop or flaunt my old credentials as a consultant, that attitude still required a switch for me. It was just a job. My priority, my focus, needed to remain at home.

I have found keeping my focus at home to be the most difficult challenge of all. The lure of my old respectability, of my old visibility and *perception* of importance, pulled hard. Old habits leapt to life. It was tempting to think I could serve two masters. Job responsibilities had a fantastic talent for looking and sounding urgent, crucial, and important. Formulating a township's fundraising plan sounds a heck of lot more life-changing than washing towels or reading a story to a child.

But it isn't.

It was important that I do my job with integrity and commitment, but my priority needed to be my home. Ladies, this is *so very hard* to do. So many things pull us away from that tight focus. They are sneaky, those pulling things, and more often than not they are good, worthy pursuits. Most mothers in this boat will tell you it is infinitely harder to work part time than it is to work full time. So many gray areas murk the waters. So many compromises lurk in the corners of our daily negotiation. The ratio of dollars earned to dollars spent on child care never fails to shave it nerve-wrackingly close.

> It was important that I do my job with integrity and com-mitment, but my priority needed to be my home.

Thinking back, I wonder if it might have been a better choice *not* to return to my old career. The good money drove a hard bargain, but the level of responsibility and the lure of old attitudes was even harder on me. Think carefully about what you do to contribute to the family income. The dollars are an important consideration, but I honestly think a slightly longer stint at a job with less pay but less stress is a valuable trade-off.

My life has been a bit of a roller coaster in this respect. My fundraising career is completely over. God chose an amazing new career for me when I was least suspecting it (this seems to be a favorite theme of his in my life).

The book that you hold in your hands is the product of this new career. God chose to lead me away from what I felt was a solid career in fundraising into the most extraordinary career I could have ever imagined. To be a published author is a fantastic blessing beyond my wildest dreams. It is, however, a difficult balancing act, filled with pitfalls and land mines. It is easy—unbeliev-ably easy—for the *perceived* glamour of my writing to pull me away from the small but precious tasks of moth-erhood. To say yes to requests that sound wonderful and would fuel my hungry ego, but cost my family more than I am ready to admit. This doesn't mean God's astounding new plan for my life is bad, just that it's hard. It is something that brings me to my knees in worry and humility often—and perhaps not often enough.

Tie Yourself to the Mast

Take a cue from the mythological hero Ulysses and tie yourself to the mast when you're sailing past the siren's song. In this epic tale, the lure of these beautiful magical singing women was stronger than any man's ability to resist. So, rather than get all egotistical about his strength of will, Ulysses tied himself to the mast so he couldn't jump ship.

Wimping out? Hardly. More like recognizing the strength of one's adversary. Grab the ropes and start tying, ladies, it is time to face the facts.

Limits—especially ones set outside of the heat of battle—are your ropes that hold you to your mast. Had Ulysses' men waited until they heard the sirens' song, they might have quickly forgotten their knot-tying skills. It is hard to say no to a tempting offer laid out in front of you. The easy virtue of "just this once." Jeff and I sat down and set limits. We plotted how much work was needed to produce the necessary income, and how many hours per month or per week that would entail. I took a sharp pruning knife to the list of chores or committees, pre-planning which would fall by the wayside while my time was divided between work and home (this one was hardest). Cut back on my church work? You bet. I practiced saying no. Have you ever thought that your stepping off a committee may be God's way of growing a new person?

Perhaps most important of all, I made the commitment to Jeff, and myself, that any breech of these limits could only be done by agreement of the whole family. Mostly I have kept to this, but I will confess I've failed and agreed to a few extra commitments now and then. And had to sheepishly apologize to my family for it.

The basic, challenging truth is that while your body and mind can go to work, your heart needs to stay home. "For where your treasure is, there shall your heart be also" (Matt. 6:21). I have some pretty alluring things that look a lot like treasures lurking outside my home. When the time came (yes, it came, but that is another story) that it was no longer a financial concern, we crafted a new measuring stick. What did we *need*, and what did I *want?* I could no longer fool anyone that I was writing to help the family bottom line. The money and visibility had to come second, become pleasant amenities to my primary role as Chief Home Officer. Greed. Ego. These are lethal adversaries to a woman's heart at home.

This was a much harder measure. It is difficult to ensure that the pleasure I derive from my writing never outweighs my ability to see to the needs of my children. Or my husband. You think it's tough to balance work on a needs basis? Try it on a "wants" basis. You learn a great deal about your weaknesses.

Having a writing career right now means I say some mighty hard "no"s. I do things that will knowingly hamper me professionally because they keep my focus on my family. Like the woman asked to cook for Elijah with the last of her oil and cornmeal, I often lay down the fact that I'm not doing what might be best business-wise so I can do what's best family-wise. I often do the job I *can*, rather than the job I'd like to, because I don't have the time or energy outside of my home commitments. And I blow it a lot—both on the home and the work fronts. Far more than I'd like to admit.

God's not done with me yet. I'm convinced he has a use for all the hard lessons I have learned in the last five years. I've learned the important lesson of valuing the transformation. For, when you think about it, until we get to Heaven, it is *all* transformation. I'm not learning how to be an at-home mom or a working mom, I'm learning to follow where God leads me. To let him mold me along the way into something I can't always quite see. And that, I'm guessing, is the point of it all.

Personal Reflections

1. How do you feel about being employed outside the home? Where are (or will be) the lures for you that might prove dangerous? Can you think of what God might call you to learn in a season of employment?

2. How will you and your family make the decision when the time comes? If you have already faced this dilemma, are you pleased with how you made your decision? What might you change?

3. IF you find your mind and body must go to work, how will you (or do you) keep your heart at home? What steps can you (or do you) take to keep your home your priority? Where do you think the pitfalls for you might be? How can you "tie yourself to the mast"?

chapter 13

The Job Description:
The High Holy Ordinary

ON EVERY JOB description I have ever had, there was this one suspicious line hiding at the bottom: "Other duties as assigned." Now, I'll admit that this may be a quirk of the not-for-profit sector, but this line has always been the spice—good and bad—of each of my jobs. It's the catch-all phrase for those odd tasks that are specific to this particular organization and this particular job. Usually, in my experience, it's code for *all that stuff we couldn't possibly put in print but you'll probably end up doing anyway.*

Sometimes these quirks have been extraordinary benefits, like driving a celebrity around town, interviewing exciting or inspiring people, or doing once-in-a-lifetime things like riding in a stunt plane. Before you turn green with envy, please know that such lush experiences are far from the norm of everyday fundraising life. Payment, perhaps, for the hundreds of times you hear "no" to a donation request. However, when you deal with inspiring causes or ritzy dinner galas, occasionally some unique fun finds its way into your job.

More often than not, though, these "other duties as assigned" were decidedly unpleasant. Climbing into the ceiling of an office to try and stop a torrential water leak. Scrubbing toilets (prophetic, don't you think?). Pest control (don't ask). Running interference for another staff member with an unruly donor ("No, sir—and I *really mean* it this time—making a large donation does *not* entitle you to a dinner date with the Executive Director").

Motherhood has had its "other duties" for me as well. Some of them have been decidedly unpleasant. I've discovered, though, that each of them is a necessary facet of my education as a mother. They've been lessons I don't think I could have learned any other way. Looking upon them as the unique aspects of my job, no matter how ... uh ... yucky, has helped me put them in perspective.

> *If character is who you are when nobody's looking, then humility is who you are when your children are staring straight at you.*

Children's honesty is one of the universe's greatest humility teachers. I'll grant you, I needed a Ph.D. in humility when I first came home. I can admit that, now, but only because of my continuing, excruciating education in the subject. Things like "Mom, you're getting puffy" (my personal favorite). "This tastes horrible." "Stevie's mom thinks you're weird." "You ate that last chocolate bar, didn't you?" If character is who you are when nobody's looking, then humility is who you are when your children are staring straight at you.

Or drooling on you. I have a distinct pre-kids memory of sitting with a friend's baby, watching the drool, and thinking "How does she stand being so messy?" *Drool?* Drool is the *easy* part. Suctioning out a newborn's nose with that dastardly bulb-like instrument—now that's getting messy. Babies are experts at the private humiliation of muck and goo.

The real lessons, though, came for me in the *public* humility.

Let's talk parasites, shall we?

My toughest lesson came in many-legged form. Ladies, you simply haven't lived a full life until you've sat under a bright lamp with your husband combing through your hair like some kind of baboon on *The Nature Channel* and heard him say—rather squeamishly—"Uh-huh, you've got 'em too." At that exact moment my only thought was "Do not throw up . . . do not throw up . . . do not throw up." The private horror of head lice is one of the war stories of motherhood—the nasty shampoo, the hundreds of loads of laundry, nights upon nights of combing every square inch of hair. The public part is doubly hard to swallow.

Our family contracted a whopping case of head lice because no one told us we had been exposed. That made me angry. Had we been alerted, we could have caught it before it infected our entire household. Yet it is easy to see how such a thing happens. It is horrible to call parents of friends and classmates and tell them your kids may have given them head lice. To listen to the uncomfortable silence on the other end of the phone. Even my anger— which made me determined not to subject another family without warning like we'd experienced—didn't ease the embarrassment. Lice isn't a hygiene indicator, it just *happens*. The essential truth was that it was in my child's best interest—and the best interest of those we'd come in contact with—that everyone knew. It wasn't about me. But it sure didn't feel that way.

I even had to speak to a mother's group the next week. I was beaten down by the endless courses of eating crow, exhausted by the dozens of laundry loads, and feeling like the cover model for *Bad Mothers Monthly*. I called a speaking colleague and she gave me wise advice. "This is when the chips are down. When it's been nasty. What you know to be true now is perhaps the most true of all. Think about what's important to you right now, and you'll know what's important in the long run."

What's most important in the long run is this: It's not about me. Time after time I'll watch my dander get up where it doesn't belong over something trivial at school or a playdate. Why? Because I think it reflects badly on me. I tell my daughter to put on another outfit when she's chosen her own clothes because *I'm* worried about how other parents view my child. I keep her from making important mistakes because I don't want to look bad. But it's not supposed to be about me.

I have learned humility in accepting that sometimes the best thing I can do for my child is to let them embarrass me. Or our whole family. To value their learning experience over my public appearance. It's like ignoring a toddler's tantrum at the mall—everyone looks at you sideways and you're sure they're reaching into their bags for cell phones to dial the Child Protection Agency, but it's still the best thing you can do.

Pigtails, Snowpants, and Other Hills to Die On

Sometimes the "not about you" has nothing to do with their mistakes. It has to do with choosing your battles and about respecting their choices. For me, this was pigtails and snowpants. When Amanda was in the second grade, there'd be mornings when we would butt heads harder than longhorn sheep in mating season. Arguments over tiny details blown way out of proportion. I insisted Amanda wear her hair up every day because it looked neater that way. She was excruciatingly particular about whether or not her pigtails (which I loved—notice I said "I" loved) were exactly at the same height. This often meant doing it four or five times to get it so she liked it. You can imagine the resulting spats.

Now really, would my child's educational experience be heightened by hairdos? No. In fact, I'm not at all sure it didn't hinder it. Pigtails simply are not worth that kind of bother. Yet we had an amazing ability to brew up a tempest in a teapot over the issue. And why? When I am truly honest with myself, it was because I perceived her—and was convinced other adults would too—as more well-groomed with her hair up.

Snowpants were the same way. Every winter morning I'd insist—because I'm the mom, and insisting is part of my job—that she'd put on her snowpants. When, in actuality, she walked a half block up a shoveled driveway and walked over perhaps three feet of snowy ground to get on the bus. She would put them on to play in the snow for recess, and she already had snowboots on in the mornings. Were snowpants really that necessary? Or did I just make them so? Was this about her legs being cold or my ability to command her?

Yes, there are times when it is absolutely essential to stand your ground. Times when you must say, "It doesn't matter what you want; we're going to do it this way." But we so often become tyrannical *just because we can*. And so often over issues that don't warrant it.

I got a huge lesson in this the other day. Amanda had done something she knew was wrong—something minor, but against my wishes all the same—because she thought it would make her look "cool" in front of a friend. After a few days of feeling awful about it, she finally came and told me. I could have yelled. I could have gotten angry. It would have been easily within my rights as a conscientious parent. After all, she had disobeyed my wishes.

Ah, but there was so much more at stake. Thankfully, God gave me the grace to see this minor infraction for what it was: A learning experience and a strengthening of her conscience. Instead of a girl who disobeyed, I was able to see her as a person learning a valuable lesson: Doing stuff just to look cool hardly ever makes you look cool, and mostly makes you feel terrible. Can you think of a more valuable lesson for a nine-year-old? Can you imagine a more tangible lesson in what your conscience is and why God gave it to you? Only through grace was I able to see past my role in this experience, to see past the issue of my authority to the far greater bond of welcoming my daughter to come to me comfortably with an error. Yes, I made sure there were consequences for her actions. But I thanked her and praised her for coming to me. And she actually thanked me for not getting angry. The strong link in our relationship forged in this instance far outweighs anything she might have learned from a punishment.

This is *Still* "My Father's World"

Even really big errors have their place. I was fired from my first job. For insubordination (I'm guessing by now that comes as not much of a surprise). You can imagine this did not make my mother proud. Even though my late father was successfully self-employed, she didn't take kindly to my wanting to throw corporate America to the wind and strike out on my own. And getting canned in your first job is not exactly pretty.

> Only through grace was I able to see past the issue of my authority to the far greater bond of welcoming my daughter to come to me comfortably with an error.

What it was, however, was the best education I ever received. I learned valuable lessons from that experience. Sure, my mom would have loved for me to avoid that experience, but the truth of the matter is that it was a worthwhile blunder. I want God to give me the grace to allow my children their worthwhile blunders. God occasionally chooses to mold his creatures through difficulty. Okay, more than occasionally.

We are not in control. Our kids fall flat on their faces. Every one of us have had those experiences where situations have conspired to an awful outcome, and we grieve, anticipating our children's spirits will be trampled in the aftermath. More often than not, however, they come away better, stronger for the experience. The strength of our parenting helps them come away better, stronger. We cannot shield them—in fact, we *shouldn't*—from their mistakes. Instead we should strengthen them.

Sounds impossible for mere mortals like us. A host of influences are ready to help us fuel fear for our children. Some of them are prudent, others are dangerous. Fifteen minutes with a newspaper is enough to send your heart puddling to the floor.

We rob our children of the greatest gift of all if we let the bad news and warnings win. And so I add to our "other duties as assigned," our lessons learned only through parenting, the following war cry: "This is *Still My Father's World.*"

Like the old hymn says, the world is still under God's sovereignty. Despite all it's bumps, bruises, and bad news, this is still a wonderful place. "That though the wrong seems oft so strong, God is the ruler yet." My job is not to shield them from My Father's World, but to shape them to be part of it. To be a force for good. To temper "stranger danger" with "every person is a child of God."

I wrote the first part of this chapter September 10, 2001. On September 11, the evil in this world reared its head in catastrophic proportions as terrorists attacked New York City, Pennsylvania, and Washington D.C. Today the "wrong seems oft so strong." And I wondered, as I headed down to my office this morning, do I still feel the world is a wonderful place?

My admittedly shaky answer must still be yes. But perhaps it is more like, "there is still wonder in the world." Tales of heroism in that horror are just now coming to light. Beside the bone-deep fear is the bone-deep conviction that the world's growing darkness needs our light that much more. "God is the ruler yet." My God is stronger than the horrors of this day. I find it a good and wonderful thing that a cousin was born into my family amidst the awful news. I cannot escape the feeling that the world needs Jesus today more than it did a week ago.

The conviction to pull my light out from underneath that bushel of fear, to be a force for good, to raise children who are forces for good so desperately needed by the world, rises high in my chest.

We kid ourselves into thinking it is we who can keep our children safe. Car seats, safety caps, nontoxic crayons, etc. But it is not us who keep our children safe. Our children are not ours—only loaned to us to raise. They belong to God, and as such fall under his mighty protection. His awesome power. They are protected in ways we cannot even begin to know. And perhaps destined to know pain such as we would never wish on anyone, to prepare them for great acts of courage and compassion.

It's almost too much to bear. How can we, frightened, unskilled mothers that we are, ensure our children's success?

We can't.

The Most Vital Lesson of All

And so for me, another "duty as assigned" is reliance. Not as in being reliable, but as in relying. Dependency. Inadequacy. Perhaps it might be more accurate to say that my children have taught me insufficiency. Or that they have taught me how to *live with my perceptions of insufficiency.* As a former executive, this one's a real thorn in my side. I continually tie myself in knots over skills I think I don't have. Control I can't get. Over decisions I must make without complete information, projects that feel beyond me (let's not even talk about third grade math), and pressures that threaten to overtake me.

One day, I was driving away from the sitters' house where, for the first time in months, CJ had not stood there crying as I left. It's an ageless story—he cries his eyes out while you're in the room and you feel your heart shatter like broken glass, only to later hear reports that he trotted off happily to the puzzles once you were out the door. It's a stage. Your brain knows that, but no one has relayed this to your heart.

This day, we had reached a milestone. For whatever reason—age, weather, what he ate for breakfast, whatever—CJ had smiled and happily waved goodbye to me as I left. I floated out of that house on a cloud. It was a day for celebration.

Now, celebration for me is pretty much synonymous with coffee. My first stop without a doubt was going to be to Dunkin' Donuts for a chocolate glazed donut and hazelnut coffee. As I drove down the road, I discovered the major obstacle to my festivities: no cash. Surely, I reasoned, there must be enough change in this car to buy coffee and a donut. So, once I pulled into the Dunkin' Donuts parking lot, I set about scouring the floor and seats of my car.

It wasn't until about ten minutes had passed that I noticed a crucial fact. Most Dunkin' Donuts have large picture window fronts. As I peered above the dashboard toward the store, my deepest fears were realized. There, inside the store, were the two salespeople staring straight at me—like they'd seen this type of thing before.

I must have looked rather pathetic. Entirely too desperate for a cup of coffee. This struck me as enormously funny. By the time I made it into the store, I could barely breathe and hold onto my hand full of change for laughing so hard. Foolishly, I tried to explain the situation, but it only made me laugh harder.

The man behind the counter had a radiant face. He knew. He just *knew*. I could tell by his eyes.

"You have a lovely smile," he said to me, smiling himself. It is perhaps one of my favorite compliments in recent memory. Then he said something that has stuck with me in deep and powerful ways. "Order whatever you want," he said, *"It'll be enough."*

It'll be enough.

It *will* be enough. That is the true secret of mother-hood. If the calls to excellence and creativity in this book have made you feel like you haven't got what it takes, if the world seems too dangerous a place, hear the deeper message I hope to give you: It'll be enough. Whatever you bring to this job is enough. And it is enough because God does the rest. Jesus takes us where we are, not where we ought to be. That gener-ous donut man became the clearest metaphor I know for what God does for me as a mother. He takes the coins I've managed to scrounge off the floor of my life and turns it in to something sufficient to the task. To something greater than I could have hoped to accomplish on my own.

> Whatever you bring to this job is enough. And it is enough because God does the rest.

Don't think terrorist, think school bus. You fully understand you're not in control when you watch the flesh of your flesh, bone of your bone, climb into the big yellow school bus and wave goodbye. Off on their own and away from us.

I hope I find you singing at the bus stop. Lifting hands in praise that you've launched tiny forces for good out into the world that needs it badly. That they are on the way to becoming whatever God has in mind for them.

Only to come home for lunch.

And the Chief Home Officer knows, to her toes, that the best "power lunches" of all nearly always involve peanut butter.

Personal Reflections

1. WHAT "other duties as assigned" have come to you through your mothering experience? What have they taught you that you could not learn any-where else?

2. CAN you remember a "worthwhile blunder" that you've experienced as you grew up? What did you learn? Have you had to sacrifice your appearance/comfort for the sake of a child's learning experience? How did it feel as a parent? If you had the chance to handle the situation differently all over again, what would you change?

3. WHAT fuels your fear for your children? Is it helpful or hampering? How might you fortify your trust in God to keep that fear in a healthy perspective?

4. FINALLY, take some time to think how reading this book has affected you. What are the big lessons you've learned? What information has been most useful? Where do you need to concentrate on improving?

I've enjoyed sharing my mothering life with you, and I hope God has brought new and exciting ideas into your life through this book. I'd love to hear from you—your stories, your struggles, where you laughed, and where you thought I was off my rocker. My contact information can be found on page 228. Thanks for carving out the time to read *Becoming a Chief Home Officer*. God Bless!

Leader's Guide

Introduction

A discussion group for moms provides a wonderful opportunity for personal growth, friendship, and encouragement. Women in the profession of motherhood can struggle with isolation if they do not have regular networking opportunities. They can feel unappreciated without a pat on the back every once in a while. And they can lose vision if they are not reminded of the importance of the job they are doing. This leader's guide is designed to stimulate the building of relationships that will encourage, equip, and educate moms. Whether your group is a small group that meets in your living room, or a larger moms' group, or MOPS group that meets in a church or community building, the most important aspect of gathering together is intentionally building relationships.

Preparing to Lead

First, pray for the women in your group and for God's guidance as you lead the group.

Take some time each week before the group meets to familiarize yourself with the discussion agenda. Make notes on additional questions you might present to the group. Create a list of items you need to remember to bring to the meeting. Consider creating a "study basket" specifically for keeping items you will need each week. Pens, highlighters, name tags, index cards, notebook paper, and your copy of the book would be basic essentials. When special items are needed for a specific week, just drop them in the basket and you'll be assured to remember them!

You'll notice that every discussion has four parts each playing an important role in meaningful interaction with the content and in relationship building. Let's take a quick look at the purpose of each part.

Icebreaker

When your group first gets together each week, you will find it beneficial to start out with a lighthearted, get-to-know-you-better activity. Each mom has probably had a hectic time just getting to the group and she may be preoccupied with thoughts of child care, household chores that are going undone, or juggling this week's carpool responsibilities or extracurricular activities. The 10–15 minute Icebreaker is designed to focus everyone on the people around them and the topic at hand. It fosters relationships and builds a sense of camaraderie through laughing and sharing together.

When you finish up the Icebreaker time, open the discussion part of your meeting with prayer. Commit your time to the Lord and ask him to lead your discussion.

Dig Deep

The best moms' groups are not led by leaders who like to hear themselves talk, but rather by leaders who draw out the thoughts of others. The questions in Dig Deep are designed to facilitate discussion rather than teach a lesson and will probably take about 30–45 minutes.

Don't feel confined by the questions listed in the leader's guide. If you believe another line of questions better fits your group, adjust the discussion to fit your group's needs. You might also refer to the personal reflection questions at the end of each chapter for further ideas.

During the group's discussion time your job will be to draw out the women. You will most likely have some women who want to monopolize the discussion and some who hardly say a word on their own. To draw out the woman who is quieter, you may find it useful to ask her some questions specifically to help her join the discussion. When a group member has the habit of monopolizing conversations, keep the discussion moving by calling on other women immediately after you pose a question. If the group gets off the subject in their discussions, simply pull the focus back to the original question posed to get back on track.

Apply

The true benefit of reading this book and discussing it with others is not to simply absorb new information, but rather to experience positive changes in daily life. The Apply section is designed to stimulate personal application and provide the opportunity for the moms to share how they have been challenged or moved to action. Some participants may want to invite one another to hold them accountable to make the changes God is impressing upon them, or commit to encouraging one another through challenging change. Others may discover life-changing implications they would have never thought of on their own. This vitally important part of the discussion may take approximately 10–20 minutes to complete.

Pray

Prayer may be either invigorating or intimidating depending on a person's understanding and experience with prayer. If the moms in your group are comfortable praying together, take some time at the end of your group to pray together about the things you have learned. As the leader, take the responsibility of closing out the prayer time when the group seems to be finished praying or when the clock requires that you end your time together.

If your group is not comfortable praying together, then close the group in prayer yourself or ask another member of the group who is comfortable praying aloud to do so. The prayer suggestions are simply suggestions. Pray whatever God lays on your heart to pray. There is no right or wrong when it comes to prayer; simply talk to God as you would talk to a friend.

Assignments and Notes

In some chapters you may find an assignment for the next week or notes to help your planning. These will help you gather together any items that might be needed in the next chapter or the coming weeks.

It is a core value of Hearts at Home to provide resources to moms, moms' groups, and moms' group leaders. We hope this book provides you the opportunity to interact with women who are doing the same job you are doing. Our goal is that this, and other Hearts at Home resources, will encourage, educate, and equip women in the profession of motherhood!

Jill Savage
Author, *Professionalizing Motherhood*
Founder and Director, Hearts at Home

Chapter One: Consider Yourself Promoted

Icebreaker

Go around the group and as the women introduce themselves, have them name one thing that has surprised
them—for better or worse—about at-home motherhood.
If you have a funny story about your own first weeks at
home, share it with the group.

Dig Deep

1. Ask each member of the group to briefly share her
   decision process of staying home (the brief part of this
   may be difficult). What do you all have in common?
   What is unique to each woman? Have the women
   share the reactions they received when they told others of their decision. Did they help or hinder?

2. Have the women share how their relationship with God
   affected the decision. Did they feel God's calling in
   their decision? Was it more centered on practical concerns? Circumstances? Has that changed since they've
   come home?

3. Ask each member to think about what in their lives has
   prepared them to decide to come home? Did they
   "feel" prepared? What aspects of at home motherhood

make each woman most uncomfortable? Which do they long for?

Apply

1. Read Psalm 16. How do these words of reassurance help you as you consider the transition you're making (or will be making) to full-time motherhood? List all the things God provides in this psalm. Which do you need most now? How can you remind yourself that God can be trusted to provide them, even when things get bumpy?

2. Have each woman make a list of the strengths they bring to motherhood. If the group knows each other well, let the women share their perceptions of each others' gifts and talents. Then have each woman do the same with her weaknesses. It may be uncomfortable for the women to share weaknesses—but you may find that all women have essentially the same fears no matter what their strengths are.

Pray

Pray that God will reveal to each woman the things he longs to teach them through their motherhood experience.

Pray for each woman's transition into at-home motherhood, that God will send her the resources, strength, and vision to be her best.

Pray for wisdom and courage as each woman begins to examine her experience as an at-home mother, and that God would bless the efforts of this study and bring forth great fruit within each family.

Have each of the women commit to praying for each member of the group at least once before the next meeting.

Chapter Two: Management Training

Icebreaker

Ask each woman to share their most embarrassing moment as a new mom. Create a game by seeing who can spell "Amoxicillin," "streptococcus," or other common pediatric foibles with tough names the fastest.

Dig Deep

1. Have the women share times where they were "beyond their ability to cope." How do they view the situation in hindsight? What did they learn from such a trial? Have someone read the familiar "Footprints" poem if you can obtain a copy (check the internet), and have each woman write a private passage of thanksgiving for having come through a trying time.

2. Talk about the obstacles each of us face in asking for help. What prevents us from asking for help when we need it? What can we, as women, do to make asking each other for help easier? What about organizations such as preschools, playgroups, or churches?

3. Have each woman share the most difficult part of her transition from work to home. Are their days full enough? Too full? How does the pace of our days measure up with what we feel might be the ideal pace? What happens to us when that pace is wrong? How can we fix it?

Apply

1. Discuss the world's view of "a successful woman." Now have each woman write her own personal concept of a successful mother at home. Invite the women to share what they've written. What places do you need to redefine your thinking?

2. Have each woman make a timeline of a common day in her life. Divide the sample day into morning, afternoon, and evening. Where are the trouble spots for each family? Are they the same for each family or different? Have each woman—or the whole group—brainstorm three things they might do to make a day go more smoothly.

3. As a group, make a list of the most difficult times/issues in the first weeks with a new baby. How can we support women in these trying times? What can we do as individuals? What about as a neighborhood small group, church, or women's ministry?

Pray

Is there a mother in crisis in your community? Pray for her. Let her know you are praying for her.

Pray for each of the children in your group. Ask God to give them compassion and tenderness toward their siblings. Ask God to give us, as mothers, the ability to recognize each child's unique needs and gifts.

Encourage each mother to lift up each day in prayer.

Chapter Three: Paychecks

Icebreaker

Tell the women they have an imaginary free hour and $100 to pamper themselves. Have each woman share what they'd do and why (by the way, there doesn't always have to be a why—some of the best indulgences are purely irrational).

Dig Deep

1. Have the women discuss their feelings about no longer contributing to the family income. Be sensitive; anything involving money can be a difficult issue. Most of us have mixed emotions—relief and fear. What do they fear most about living on a single income?

2. Have the women discuss attitudes of abundance vs. attitudes of scarcity. Where do these attitudes come up in your life? What decisions have you made out of scarcity that might have changed completely if you viewed the world with abundance?

Apply

1. Read the story of the ten virgins from Matthew 25:1-13. What lesson is there in this story for us when we fail to invest in our own needs? No bridegrooms are coming to our house in the middle of the night, but what bigger

issues or events come upon us suddenly and wreak havoc? How can we "keep watch"?

2. Have each woman make a list of ten little indulgences that make her happy. Have each woman identify how much each costs. Make a commitment to try at least two before you meet again and see what happens.

3. Compare and contrast how a wife's spending habits/money values might differ with those of her husband. Where are they similar? Where are some of the differences? Where do the differences tend to create tension?

4. Have each woman complete the following sentences: Money bought me_____. That purchase brought me_____. Let each woman privately explore as many discretionary/luxury items as she wants. Invite the women to share insights on what the answers reveal about how women might use money to affirm themselves.

Pray

Have each woman commit her finances to the Lord. Let each woman offer up areas of thanksgiving and lift up areas of concern in silence or aloud. Commit to praying for each other in financial matters.

Pray that God changes our vision of money from "end in itself" to "tool."

Chapter Four: Time Off

Icebreaker

How do you "get away?" Is it a bubble bath? Locking yourself in the bathroom? Large amounts of chocolate? What's the most outrageous thing you've done when the kids pushed you over the edge?

Dig Deep

1. Talk about the guilt many women associate with getting away from their children. Where does that come from? How can we counteract it? What are the consequences of putting our children ahead of our spouses and our own welfare?

2. Read Deuteronomy 5:12–15 and Genesis 2:1–3. Discuss why the Sabbath is part of the Ten Commandments. What value do we place ahead of rest when we disobey this commandment?

3. Talk about a woman's time away from her family. What makes it good? What makes it bad? How do you know you've got enough—or too little, or too much?

Apply

1. Revisit the Ten Commandments in Deuteronomy 5. Observe how much attention is paid to rest in verses 12–15. Why do you think this command has so much detail in it? Why do you think God commanded the Sabbath to be held as holy? Try rewriting verses 12–15 for your own life. What long list of things would be in verse 14?

2. Look at a day broken down into hourly slots. Have the women rate the hours from difficult to easy. Where are the straining times? Would a session of rest before that time help? Where might times of rest be inserted?

3. Have each woman make a list of what each member of their family might need from a vacation. Then compare the last vacation they took to that list. Were needs met?

What kind of vacation might meet those needs more effectively?

4. Have the women share experiences about getting away with their husbands. What worked? What didn't? What options are there when grandparents aren't a readily available child care option?

Pray

Thank God for the gift of rest. Pray for the wisdom to know when we need rest and lift up each woman's need for time away. Pray that God would clear obstacles and provide resources so that each woman can find the rest she needs.

Pray for each woman's marriage. Ask God's help in making the marriage relationship a priority in her home. Pray that husbands would be as willing to make the logistics work as the wife. Ask that God bless the time they carve out alone together and commit to pray for each woman's time away.

Have each woman get out her calendar, planner, etc. and lay it on the table. Pray over them. Commit each woman's days to the Lord, their planning to his will, their daily tasks to his service. Ask that God nurture and bless us not only to serve, but to thrive.

Chapter Five: Career Clothes

Icebreaker
If someone said you must live in the same outfit for a week, which outfit would it be? Why? Do you have a favorite "comfort" item of clothing? What is it about it that appeals to you?

Dig Deep
1. Have the women discuss how they feel appearance effects their mothering. Recognize the differences— for some women the impact will be much stronger. Discuss the difference between taking care with our appearance and becoming overly concerned with it. Where does self care slip into vanity?

2. Discuss the "flags of defiance" Allie talks about in her red lipstick and bright nail polish. Do the women agree or disagree? What might be their own "flags"? Would it be something they already own, or would it have to be something bought just for that use?

3. Have the women share how they shop for clothes now that they are at home mothers. What has changed? What's better now? What's worse? What do they miss from their working wardrobes? How have finances affected how they shop?

Apply

1. Read Psalm 139:14. When was the last time you felt "wonderfully made"? When was the last time you treated yourself as "wonderful"? Helped yourself to remember it? What in how you maintain your appearance would help you remember it? What hinders your remembering?

2. Have the women think about the last item of clothing they bought for themselves. Was it practical or an indulgence? How long has it been? How would they rate the time and energy spent on their appearances vs. what they spend on the appearance of their children?

3. Have each woman share a "hint." Anything from "how to get mascara on while holding a baby" to "why men's T-shirts are cheaper than women's." Have the women share their favorite place to shop and why.

4. If you think the women might find this fun, bring several bottles of bright red nail polish and have at it. If

nothing else, bring a bottle of really wonderful hand cream and pass it around.

Pray

Ask that God give each woman a right spirit about her appearance. To know the right balance between inner beauty and external appearance. Pray to have eyes to see beauty in others, and compliment them in ways that will lift their spirits.

Pray for women facing image issues such as mastectomies, those with disfigurements, loss of limbs, or burn victims. Ask that God give these women a special sense of their inner beauty and that they be protected from insensitive comments. Pray the same for children facing similar issues.

Pray for the grace to face our aging bodies wisely. For wisdom to know that our spiritual health is always our first concern. Praise God for the wonder of our bodies, and ask his protection over each woman's health and well being as she cares for her children and husband.

Chapter Six: Raises, Praises, and Promotions

Icebreaker

Have the women share a "burnt breadstick" story, where a seemingly minor infraction has been worsened by a child's or spouse's comment. Ask the women if they could laugh about it then, or if they could only fume. Is it funny now?

Dig Deep

1. Select two or three Bible passages that reflect God's love for his people. Have the women paraphrase it to fit a mother's situation at home. Let each woman share what speaks to her heart in the passage.

2. Discuss "ordinary." What feels ordinary to each woman? Where does she feel her work goes particularly unnoticed? Be honest about how the lack of visibility effects our morale as mothers. What ways can we refocus our thinking so that it does less harm?

3. Ask the women to share times when burn out and frustration were high. What happened? What were the consequences? What could have been done to avoid it?

Apply

1. Read Naaman's story in 2 Kings 5. What are your "wash in the Jordan"s? How can you recast them in a light that reflects your service to God? Who can best serve as your "servant," reminding you what it is you are truly being asked to do?

2. Have the women write down ten things they need to do each week. Share the lists, and see how many of them are "task" oriented (it will most likely be 90% if not 100%). Now have each woman write a second list, compiling ten things they can do to nourish their families. Discuss how to make room for both in a woman's week.

3. Have the women identify three outstanding seasoned mothers in your community. Why not have them come share their wisdom—what better praise and encouragement is there?

4. If the group is well-enough acquainted, have each woman write two positive comments about every woman in the group. Share them.

Pray

Pray that each woman hears God's loving, praising voice in her daily life. Ask for ears to hear, eyes to see the praises God gives her though her children and husband.

Give thanks for each woman in the group, naming her gifts and talents. Give thanks for being together and ask that a spirit of encouragement fill the group both now and in the future.

Pray for moms alone, without support and encouragement. Ask that God bring each of you to the side of a woman who needs help, and that God's call to help will be heard.

Chapter Seven: Training and Development

Icebreaker
Have each woman write a paragraph describing how she thought her life would be at home before she stopped working. What's come true? What hasn't? What's better than she expected? Worse?

Dig Deep
1. Discuss how mothers need training. There's no "mommy school," so how do we learn? What doesn't get taught that should? Let each woman share what skills and strengths she brought into her new role at home, and what skills she feels she's lacking. Talk about the feelings associated with those missing skills. Are they helpful or do they hinder us getting help?

2. Have the women share what's "urgent" in their days and what's "important." How do we fight the "urgent" to get to the "important"? Do families have rules, rituals, or traditions that help? How can we, as mothers, keep our focus on the "important"?

3. Give the women some quiet time to reflect—in writing, if possible—about where God might be calling their personal growth while at home. Share within the group if it is appropriate. Why is it so easy to push our inner lives aside in all the tasks of keeping a home? How can we combat that?

Apply

1. Read Jeremiah 29:11–13. What might God's plans for you be? How has he promised in these verses to be beside you as you seek his plan? What things come to mind when you hear the words "hope and a future"? How does reading these verses convince you God wants good things for you in this season of your life?

2. Have each woman make a list—as long as she likes—of the kinds of things she'd like to do if she "had the time." Encourage the women to be unrealistic, to dream big. Share the list among the group. Are there similarities that a group effort can help to make happen? Is there something one member can teach another? Pick one thing off each woman's list and brainstorm how she might get a start in making that dream a reality. Have each woman commit to taking one small step in that direction before the next meeting. Plan to share the results when you meet again.

Pray

Pray for each woman's personal growth as a mother, as a Christian, and as a woman. Ask that God give each woman a clear sense of where he would like each one to grow. Ask that he send into each life the people and resources who can make that growth happen.

Thank God for his extraordinary knowledge of us. Praise him for his creation of each of our talents—both those we know now, and those we'll discover in the future. Rejoice in the person each of us will be when we finally reach our eternal Home.

Pray for the skills and talents of our children. That we may pass along those they enjoy, learning together as parent and child. Ask God to help us recognize the unique gifts he has given our children and give us wisdom to nurture those gifts.

Chapter Eight: Colleagues and Coworkers

Icebreaker

Have each woman share three things they'd do with a best friend but *not* a husband. Jumpstart the conversation, if need be, with some examples like (1) bathing suit shopping, (2) get your eyebrows waxed, or (3) watch *It's a Wonderful Life* for the fourteenth time—and still cry.

Dig Deep

1. Discuss the isolation mothers often feel. What circumstances feed that isolation? What can be done to reduce it? Why do we "hunker down" when things get tough instead of reaching out? Are there things your group, your church, or your neighborhood can do to encourage mothers to reach out?

2. Have the women discuss the "Myth of Not Working." Do they agree with the idea or disagree? What is the fine line between being grateful for being able to stay home, and glossing over the tough challenges we face by staying home?

3. Have each woman share a time when friendships became her lifeline. How have those relationships benefited from that time?

Apply

1. Read Hebrews 10:23–25. Are we "in the habit" of giving up on meeting together? Why? What's the cost? How can we fix it?

2. Have each woman create their own ideal "staff of friends." Would the five friends be the same as Allie's list, or different? What would each woman change about her circle of friends if she could? What steps can she take to make those changes happen?

3. Have the women think about the last time things got really tough. What steps did she take to get support from friends? Is her first impulse always the best one (i.e., eating Chocolate Fudge Ripple instead of calling a friend)? How can we train ourselves to do healthy things when the going gets tough? Think of five things and post them on a cabinet door, medicine cabinet, or near the telephone.

4. Have each woman make a list of four things she can do to nurture her existing friendships. Aim for doing one a week for the next month. Commit to doing at least one before you meet again.

Pray

Thank God for the group brought together to study this book. Thank him for the time you spend together and the relationships nourished by discussion and sharing. Let each woman thank God for a friend she has.

Pray that our friendships strengthen and increase. Ask God to give us wisdom in choosing our friendships, sensitivity to hear his call to befriend a new woman, and the willingness to go beyond our comfort zones with friends old and new.

Pray for mothers who feel friendless. For those in new communities, under hardships, serving as missionaries, or simply too weighed down by life's demands. Ask God to send them a companion mother for strength and support.

Chapter Nine: Sick Days

Icebreaker
Ask the women to name a sick-day crisis that was the most challenging. What was worst about it? Can they laugh about it now?

Dig Deep
1. Ask each woman to recount an instance where their child showed compassion to them or a sibling. How does injury or illness give us opportunities to care for each other? Can the women name any positive outcomes from times when family members were sick?

2. Have each woman share one of her "awful truths" about parenting. Why do we like to think we can avoid these? What do they teach us? How does our Christian viewpoint help us with suffering—physical and emotional?

3. Discuss the challenges of nutrition and exercise for at-home mothers. What keeps us from attending to our own bodies? Is it more attitude or circumstances? Have the group share obstacles they face and solutions they have found. How do the women feel about putting a child in "babysitting" to attend a church function, health class, or other similar event?

Apply

1. You knew this was coming: Read Proverbs 31:10–31. Before this biblical Wonder Woman sends your self esteem into the basement (who could live up to this gal?), note how many verses are devoted to her planning (15, 18, 21, 27). What can we learn from her?

2. Ask each woman to privately write down what she had for breakfast (and lunch, if applicable) that day. Rate the nutrition value (good, poor, fair) of the meal(s). Rate the enjoyment factor. Invite them to share their observations. How many of the women agree they need to take better care of their nutritional needs?

3. Talk about the value of a "sick day pact." Would it work for some women? Have the group brainstorm at least ten things they can do to be better prepared for illness in their home. Let each woman commit to two she will implement before the next meeting.

4. Ask each woman to bring a favorite recipe to the next meeting. Recipes must be nutritious, child-friendly, and easy to prepare. If members of the group have favorite cookbooks, ask them to share those as well.

Pray

Praise God as our creator, as the crafter of our bodies. Thank him for the physical trials we face as well as the health we enjoy. Pray for the health and well-being of each member of the group, as well as her children.

Pray that each woman will have the wisdom to act wisely when health concerns strike her home. Pray that God will send helpers when needed, patience when called for, and endurance to face long nights with sick children.

Pray for the health and safety of each woman's spouse or extended family they rely on for support.

Chapter Ten: Managing Your Staff

Icebreaker

Have each woman create a fictional, somewhat silly staff title for each of her children, such as Director of Food Displacement, Chief Giggle Exporter, or Vice President of Whining and Procrastination. Encourage, if need be, that each child get two titles—one positive and one negative.

Dig Deep

1. Examine a mother's relationship with and feelings toward time. Where is it our friend? Where is it our foe? See if as a group you can identify some of the characteristics of "bad" time vs. "good" time. Are these things we as mothers can control or not?

2. Let each woman share an instance where she "pulled rank" as a mother. Looking back, was it a wise choice or one she regrets? How does each woman know when to be authoritative and when to be flexible? Are there ways to repair bad choices in that area?

3. Examine how each woman's children view time. What do babies need? Toddlers? Preschoolers? Elementary schoolers? Would the children benefit from a visual timeline like Allie's, or are there other ways to help

them grasp the concept? Share what has worked and where each woman still has challenges.

Apply

1. Revisit Psalm 139, paying close attention to the opening verses. How does it help you to know that God knows both you and your children so well? Which verses give you permission to come to God with even the tiniest of problems? Where do you see awesome power to battle the big problems? Does such an inspiring picture of creation help you to see your children with new respect? What about yourself as their God-given parent?

2. Have each woman take a typical day and divide it up into "chunks" that work for her. Is the routine working? Does she need more structure? Less structure? See if there are common threads between the women of the group, or lessons to be learned from how we each manage our days.

3. Let each woman pick one area of her life where more planning is needed. Give the group some time to start examining the problems individually. Then come together to share the challenges and some solutions that have come to light. Brainstorm together if there are common issues among the women.

4. Have each woman list five values she'd like to instill as a parent. Use Allie's measuring sticks of what she admires and what drives her crazy in adults. See if, with a little examination, each woman can pick the two most important. Have each woman commit to spending some time before the next meeting thinking about those values and how they can be her focus as a mother.

Pray

Pray for sensitivity to our children's needs and learning styles. Pray for the vision to see their gifts and the wisdom to know how to give their unique personalities the proper focus.

Read Psalm 32. Pray that God will grant each mother an ideal, a vision for her parenting. Ask him to clear a time in her week to allow her to think about motherhood's bigger issues. Pray that we, as mothers, will always remember to turn to him for guidance.

Take some time to pray over the details of daily life. Potty training, loose teeth, scuffles with a classmate or teacher, or tantrums. God is as eager to share the tiny details as he is to share the bigger issues.

Chapter Eleven: Advanced Labor Relations

Icebreaker
Have each woman share an embarrassing, awful, or just plain dumb moment from a grocery store or car trip. Laugh about it if you can; commiserate if you can't.

Dig Deep
1. Let each woman share a personal attitude or fear she wishes her children had not seen. In what places do our attitudes about things negatively predispose our children? In what ways can our attitudes help the way they view the world? Are there ways to change the negative attitudes?

2. Explore the circumstances that keep mothers from planning. How can they be helped? How can we as mothers plan when we don't feel creative enough to find a solution? Where might prayer fit in to such a situation?

3. Have the women evaluate Allie's strategies. Would they work for their families? Where do they agree and disagree with Allie's approach? How would they handle the three situations—or other situations that cause their families trouble?

Apply

1. Read Philippians 4:6–7. What key to "advanced labor relations" is given here? Why does anxiety prevent clear thinking? What have you learned that may help you use prayer as your first act in facing parenthood's bigger challenges?

2. Have the woman pick another situation where an attitude shift might change something from a "chore" to an "outing." Some examples might be a trip to the doctor's office, doing homework, picking Dad up from the train station every night, etc. Work together to fashion strategies. Encourage the women to get creative and unusual.

Pray
Give thanks for the creativity—hidden and recognized—in each woman in the group. Ask him to nourish those gifts and help each woman to find new gifts.

Pray God would give each woman a right attitude no matter what the circumstances. Ask for the grace to see a challenge as an opportunity. Ask for the humility to know when we have pushed our family too far in the name of good intentions.

If there is a woman facing travel, pray for her and her family. Commit to covering her trip in prayer. Make sure she reports back how that prayer worked in her ventures!

Chapter Twelve:
Downsizing Even in the Best of Families

Note: This is a chapter that must be handled sensitively. Family finances are often charged with emotion. Take extra care.

Icebreaker
Have each woman share about their professional life "before kids." What did they enjoy about their jobs? What was bad about them? Would they return to that career if they needed to contribute to the family income for a season?

Dig Deep
  1. Have each woman share a situation (ideally not an economic one) where she had to "step out in faith." How did it feel? What did she learn from the experience?

2. Explore the group's honest feelings about mothers returning to work. How many of them feel it may be in their future one day? What are their fears? What seems attractive about it?

3. How do we, as mothers, reconcile our trust in God's provision with a hard economic reality? How does our current society muddle the issue further? What is gained when Chief Home Officers view their employment outside the home as "a temporary measure?"

Apply
1. Joseph's story in Genesis chapters 37–48 is one of the greatest "reinventing all over again" stories the Bible has to offer. Take some time to read this dramatic tale and see how Joseph learned to follow God through adversity and unexpected new roles. Can you see how God was molding Joseph to be the great leader that he was? What parallels can you draw in your own life? How can you draw strength from Joseph's trials?

2. Have each mother identify three or four issues that would face her if she needed to return to work (or have her list the issues she's facing if she's currently working). Have her privately evaluate how well she might cope (or is coping) with each one. Where are the pitfalls? What can be done now or in advance of them? Where are the blessings? What might keep us from seeing them?

3. Have each woman think about what was "not her finest hour as a Child of God." What circumstances drove her to that point? What use did God make of that dark time? What truth was eventually discovered that brought her out of it? How did she eventually know that God had not left her? How has her faith changed as a result?

4. What experiences has each woman had that she could draw from if and when she returned to work? Have her make a list of the challenges she's overcome to remind her of her own strength, and God's strengthening of her. Often just recalling these experiences gives us the fortitude we need to face challenges. How can we remind each other to offer support and encouragement?

Pray

Begin by thanking God for his provision in each woman's life. Offer up praise for the provision that has allowed each woman to be at home with her children. Give thanks for the family breadwinners that make it possible. Ask for the grace to always see the glass as "half full."

Pray that God will stay close to us whenever a season of employment arises. Ask for guidance in decisions, for him to lay good opportunities at our feet, and for wisdom in knowing our situations.

Pray that each family will keep its hearts at home. Pray for strength and encouragement for single mothers and others who must work. Ask that God use each of us as a support and encouragement to families in economic crisis.

Chapter Thirteen: The Job Description

Icebreaker

Ask each woman to name the most valuable thing she's learned from the book and the thing she most disagrees with. Are there any places where her concepts have changed over the course of the study?

Dig Deep

1. Have the group make a list of the "other duties as assigned" they'd add to the job description. Why? What do they teach us as mothers? Why is motherhood at home the best place to learn it?

2. Explore humility vs. self-esteem in motherhood. How do we achieve the right balance? What humbles each woman about her job as an at-home mother? What lifts her up and affirms her? Is it different for each woman, or are there similarities in the group?

3. Have each woman share "the control freak" inside her. In what area does a lack of control most bother her? How do we as mothers cope with lack of control? As Christians? What are good responses? Bad ones?

Apply

1. Read Psalm 145 aloud. Let the words sink in as the balm for worried souls that it is. Pay special attention to verses 18–20. You can claim this prayer not only for yourself, but for those you love. Remind yourself that God is near to you in every aspect of your transformation and growth as a mother. Let the passages give you strength and hope as you take them as the promises they are—especially, individually, perfectly for you.

2. Have each woman go through the "Job Benefits" compiled by Allie and rate them in terms of importance. Which ones matter to her most? Which matter least? Where does she need the most work to improve? Where are her strengths so she can encourage others?

3. Write a help-wanted ad for the job of Chief Home Officer. See if you can create an ad that would convince your daughter to follow in your footsteps.

4. Take considerable time to reflect as a group on the journey you have taken in exploring this book. What's been valuable? What hasn't? Where have you felt God speaking to you? How has it changed your view of the women with whom you have shared this experience?

Pray
Pray that the journey is far from over. Thank God for his ongoing transformation of our lives. Ask for the grace to listen, the strength to persevere, and the vision to improve.

Pray for the next generation. Pray that those children growing up in abundance use their blessings wisely. Pray that those growing up in scarcity overcome their obstacles to become strong forces for good. Pray for specific children in crisis if you know of any. Pray that each woman's child grows to become a godly man or woman who impacts the world in great and marvelous ways.

Give thanks for your group, for the time you've shared, and for the relationships begun or strengthened. Give thanks for the honesty and encouragement of each woman, and ask that God give each of you hearts to support each other.

Dear Reader,

Us CHIEF HOME Officers need to stick together, don't you think?

I'd like very much to hear from you about your experience reading this book. What worked for you? What didn't? Did you read it in a group? On your own? What do you wish was covered? Anything you're sure you never want to hear about again? And, of course, I love to hear any great stories you have to tell.

In a perfect world, I'd sit down with each one of you over a cup of coffee and talk for hours. Okay, that's not exactly possible, but we do have blessings like websites and email, letters and phones to keep in touch. It's great fun for me to come speak to moms' groups about the CHO philosophy and share our foibles of the parenting profession.

So please, contact me. Whether it's to talk about my coming to speak, to tell a story, or to just plain chat, I'd really enjoy hearing from you.

Here are all the ways you can reach me:

Mail: P.O. Box 7026
          Villa Park, IL 60181
Email: alliepleiter@aol.com
Website: www.alliepleiter.com

God bless you and your families,

Allie

Hearts at Home ®

The Hearts at Home organization is committed to meeting the needs of women in the profession of motherhood. Founded in 1993, Hearts at Home offers a variety of resources and events to assist women in their jobs as wives and mothers.

Find out how Hearts at Home can provide you with ongoing education and encouragement in the profession of motherhood. In addition to this book, our resources include the Hearts at Home magazine, the Hearts at Home devotional, and our Hearts at Home website. Additionally, Hearts at Home events make a great getaway for individuals, moms' groups, or for that special friend, sister, or sister-in-law. The regional conferences, attended by over ten thousand women each year, provide a unique, affordable, and highly encouraging weekend for the woman who takes the profession of motherhood seriously.

Hearts at Home
900 W. College Avenue
Normal, Illinois 61761
Phone: (309) 888-MOMS
Fax: (309) 888-4525
E-mail: hearts@hearts-at-home.org
Web: www.hearts-at-home.org

Would you like additional resources for your group?

We hope your moms' group has enjoyed reading *Becoming a Chief Home Officer.* If you would like to enhance this learning opportunity by providing your group additional mothering resources, copy this page, fill in the information, and mail or fax it to Hearts at Home. Your sample resources (magazines, devotionals, and more!) are free of charge and will arrive within 3–6 weeks. (The form is also available on our website.)

Additionally, Hearts at Home maintains a comprehensive database of moms' groups in the United States. This allows us to operate as a clearinghouse for information about the groups. For instance, if a woman moves to a new community, she can contact Hearts at Home to locate a group in her area. If you would like to be part of the Moms Group Referral Network, please indicate below.

****

☐ Yes! Please send me resources for my group!

Please ship to: _____

(Shipping address) _____

City _____ State _____ Zip _____

Contact name and phone number (____)_____

How many women regularly attend your group? _____

☐ Yes! Please include our group in your referral network!

Name of group _____

Meeting address _____

City _____ State _____ Zip _____

Contact name and phone number (____)_____

Contact email (if applicable)_____

Group website (if applicable) _____

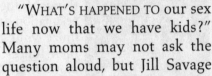